SHE LOVED THE CHURCH

SHE LOVED THE CHURCH

MOTHER JULIA VERHAEGHE

and the Beginnings of The Spiritual Family The Work

edited by
Mother Katharina Strolz, FSO
Fr Peter Willi, FSO

FAMILY PUBLICATIONS

Original title: Sie liebte die Kirche. Mutter Julia Verhaeghe
und die Anfänge der geistlichen Familie "Das Werk"
©2005 Die geistliche Familie "Das Werk"
www.thework-fso.org

Translated by Ian Logan
© 2009 The Spiritual Family The Work

ISBN 978-1-871217-87-2

Published by

Family Publications, Denis Riches House
66 Sandford Lane, Oxford OX1 5RP, UK
www.familypublications.co.uk

Printed in Malta through
s|s|media ltd

My joy is God, the threefold holy one.

Mother Julia

TABLE OF CONTENTS

The apostle Paul,
Patron of The Spiritual Family The Work

Presentation of the English Edition

The Holy Spirit is at work in the Church today and he works in many ways through many people. One of the signs of the life of the Church is the growth of new forms of consecrated life. The book that you have before you relates how one of these new forms developed in the Church because of someone who was open to God's call, someone who loved the Church and was willing to leave everything behind to be free for God's plan with her life and to co-operate with him for the good of the Church.

This portrayal of Mother Julia Verhaeghe's life with the description of the development of the charism of The Spiritual Family The Work was first published in German and later in four other European languages. The way it has been received not just by members and friends of *The Work*, but also by people who have a general interest in the life of the Church and in its impact on society, encouraged us to offer the English translation to Family Publications in Oxford. At a time when we experience a gradual re-awakening or a strengthening of the sense of the Church and a rediscovery of her spiritual riches, especially the beauty and the life-giving strength of Mass and of Eucharistic Adoration, *She loved the Church* is an encouraging example of how the Holy Spirit distributes his gifts today for the Mystical Body of Christ.

In this book we frequently use the Greek term *charism* with its rich biblical and theological content. Every charism is a special grace granted by God to an individual member of the faithful for the benefit of the Church. Jesus Christ wants to present her to himself *"in splendour, without spot or wrinkle or any such thing, that she might be holy and without blemish."* (Eph 5:27) St Paul speaks here in powerful words about the glory and the beauty of the Church. Jesus Christ loves the Church. She is the fruit of his death and of his resurrection and was revealed by the Holy Spirit at Pentecost. At all times the Holy Spirit has granted the Church specific charisms so that she could fulfil her universal mission to proclaim Christ as the Redeemer in a changing world. Among the great variety of charisms, there is the specific one to found a new community in the Church. Such a charism was granted to Julia Verhaeghe. By this special grace she became the foundress and the spiritual Mother of The Spiritual Family The Work.

The reader learns how the Lord prepared Mother Julia for her vocation and mission, how the charism became more and more her life, and how it assumed the form of an ecclesial family. The authors comply with Mother Julia's explicit wish that her biography should always be closely related to the charism of The Work, consequently the more The Work takes shape the less is said about her life. She remains however vividly present to the end of the book, as quotations from her letters are used to describe the development of The Work or to convey her deep insights into specific situations.

Mother Julia's keen faith made her appreciate the sacraments of the Church, above all the Holy Eucharist, as the inmost source of her life. It was therefore a day of great significance for her, when for the first time the Eucharistic Lord took up residence in a house of The Work in October 1950. From then onwards, it was clear that Christ's presence in the tabernacle was the centre of the community. The main part of the book ends at this momentous point in the development of The Work. With other members of The Work, Mother Katharina Strolz is engaged in further research. In 2008 she handed over her international responsibility for the Sisters of The Work to her successor, in order to be able to devote herself mainly to the spiritual heritage of Mother Julia and describe events from 1950 onwards.

Pope John Paul II characterized the mission of our Spiritual Family, referring to one of the signs of our times: "*The Church is the great work of God. If her divine origin is questioned at times today, The Work contributes to the understanding and living of the mystery of the Church in its profundity.*"[1] Through our lives, people should have the chance to realize that the Church is the dwelling place of the living Christ in this world. There we meet him. Though important and helpful ecclesial documents and voluminous theological books explain the nature and the life of the Church, it also takes living communities to bear witness to what the Church is about.

In the worldwide family of the Church, it is the charism of The Work to be a spiritual family that in various ways reflects her inner nature. Her

---

[1] See Message of Pope John Paul II to the Spiritual Family The Work, p. 197 of this book.

focus on Christ and on his unity with the Father and the Holy Spirit is reflected in the Holy Covenant which binds the members to the Heart of Jesus, and in the priority that is given to Mass and to Eucharistic Adoration in daily life. Her unity in the diversity of vocations is lived in The Work as the complementarity of the priests' community with the Sisters' community, whose members live the three evangelical counsels in close co-operation as one religious family in worship and work.

Their endeavour to live unity as their realization of a living faith, that brings forth hope and becomes visible in works of love, is supported by the harmony of a contemplative and at the same time apostolic life, which works as leaven in the world. The last aspect marks especially the members in a wider sense and the associates who come from all walks of life, families and single people. Wherever they live and work, they live up to their specific calling in the strength of the same charism, in complementarity with the consecrated members and with each other. Whether clerics or lay people, families or single people, they strive to glorify God by their faithfulness and their loyalty to the Church in the actual circumstances of their lives.

The name The Work refers primarily to the work of Christ, which the Son of God accomplished (Jn 17:4). He came into the world to glorify the Father and to free mankind from sin and death. His great work of salvation continues in the Church. Secondly, the name reminds us of the fact that all the baptized are to participate in this work through a life of faith in Christ (cf. Jn 6:29). In England, Ireland and the United States members of our Spiritual Family do that by glorifying the Triune God in their daily prayer life and by their manifold service at home or in an office, by their commitment and work in parishes, by caring for guests on retreat, by teaching at universities or by catechising children, by sharing the faith in personal contact with priests, families and single people, young and old, and last but not least by their work to make the life and teachings of John Henry Cardinal Newman better known.

Witnessing to the working of God in our times, and thus to the vitality of the Church, this book contains sayings of Mother Julia, which have already given light and help to many. The number of those who have an intimate relationship with her or who trust in her intercession is growing day by day. May this publication help those who read it to grow in love for Our Lord and for his Church, as would be Mother

Julia's wish and prayer. In this Year of St Paul, we entrust this intention to him, our patron.

Without the generous help of wonderful friends, this publication would not have been possible. We are greatly indebted to Dr Ian Logan, who generously gave his time and expertise to produce a fine translation from the German original. We thank him for his friendship and kindness. We also express our gratitude to Fr John Saward for the translation of Leo Cardinal Scheffczyk's personal testimony.

Finally we thank Colin Mason for having taken on the book on behalf of Family Publications. We deeply appreciate his careful and constructive advice in the preparation of the English edition.

MOTHER MARGARETE BINDER, FSO   FR PETER WILLI, FSO, RECTOR

25th January 2009,
Solemnity of the Conversion of St Paul

JOSEPH CARDINAL RATZINGER

POPE BENEDICT XVI

Homily at the Mass of Thanksgiving
for the Papal Approval of
The Spiritual Family The Work

Rome, St Peter's Basilica, 10 November 2001

Dear Brothers and Sisters in the Lord!

Today in the great thanksgiving of the Holy Eucharist we include the special thanksgiving for the approbation of the Spiritual Family The Work as a community of Pontifical right. Thus it is fully situated in the heart of the Church and at the same time opened up to the universal Church as a gift of the Holy Spirit, as a way forward for today and into tomorrow.

It was a dark time, when Mother Julia planted this modest seed in the earth of the Church in January 1938. When we speak of this beginning, we have to always remind ourselves that she said: *"I have founded nothing. Since Christ founded the Church everything has been founded. It is only necessary that people live this foundation profoundly, that is, on and from the foundation which Jesus himself laid."*

In fact, she didn't put another work next to the work of Jesus Christ, but gave herself totally to His work. Thus she invites all of us, not to put our own works next to the work of Christ, but to give ourselves to His work, to be in His work and to live with His work, and thus through Him, with Him and in Him to serve the salvation of the world. Everything she did relates to Christ, the Son of the living God.

And she knew that Christ is not a figure of the past, but that he lives forever in His Church. Communion with Christ is therefore communion with Him where alive he walks through the ages – in the community of the Church. And again, she knew that the sign of the Church is the Petrine ministry, that where Peter is the Church is, and that whoever wants to be in the Church and with Christ, must be close to Peter. So she leads us to the Saint of today, to Pope St Leo the Great, who in his own way also taught what her message was.

In troubled times, from 440 to 461, Leo the Great led the Church. It was the time of the fall of the western Roman Empire, the time of the great migration, the onslaught of the Huns under Attila and of the Vandals under Geiserich. In such a time Leo carried the light of faith. The greatest crisis of faith during his time was of a political-military nature; at the root of every political crisis there is a spiritual crisis. That was also the case in Leo's time. Certainly the Church after Constantine was free. The emperors were Catholic and promoted the Church. Nevertheless with this new freedom came also new dangers, new temptations.

The first temptation consisted in the submission of the Church and the faith to political power, in the exploitation and use of the Church for power, in the use of the faith for political purposes. The emperor Constantius once said: *"I am the law of the Church."* This expresses a profound temptation to falsification of the faith, which in fact did degenerate to a means of political power.

The second temptation was of an ideological nature and consisted in the adaptation of the faith to the intellectual trends of the time. It is called the hellenisation of the faith, that is a conforming of the gift of God, of the light of Revelation, to that which the people of that time thought and wanted. With the great Greek philosophy it was said: God cannot truly have a son; this is a mythological idea. God is far away. God cannot go out of himself, and the great sons of God are simply great men, just as is Jesus. He is not really the son of God. He is a great man of religious and human history. In the fifth century, the century of Pope Leo, the mystery of the Triune God and the divine sonship of Jesus was accepted after the first great Councils, but then people tried other ways of adapting it to their own mode of thinking. They said on the one hand, Christ is not entirely man, he has a divine nature only. On the other hand others said, Christ is entirely man, he only attained divinity during his life. The mystery was rethought according to human standards in order to make it understandable. But precisely because of that, the great, the new and totally other which God's revelation gave to us was lost.

In the face of this great temptation, St Leo, enlightened by the wisdom of the faith, put the truth of divine revelation on the lamp stand – that Truth which gives us life and forms the foundation of a good life and a good death. St Leo the Great was above all a teacher of Christology for the great Council of Chalcedon. He found the formulation of the dogma, and the fathers of the Council gave their consent to his letter with the words: *"Peter has spoken through Leo"*. And indeed: against the sophism of human thinking, this letter expresses the depth and simplicity of the true faith. Leo said with Peter: *"You are the Messiah, the Son of the living God."*

With the formulation of this dogma in which the true Godhead and true humanity of Christ shine equally forth, St Leo did not discover anything new, he did not create any new ideas. Just the opposite; he invited us to enter into that great light which God gave us and he showed us that light anew. Faith in Christ is at the heart of the person and the message of St Leo the Great. Only in his love for Christ, in his being permeated by the love of Christ was he able to grasp the mystery in its profundity and give again to Christ the kind of service Peter gave. Thus the Petrine mystery in this confession, which is the rock of the Church, is made present again: *"You are the Messiah, the Son of the living God."*

The primacy of Christology, the primacy of the love of Christ and of the faith in Christ is the nucleus of the message of St Leo the Great. Of course, this primacy of Christology, this preeminence of the faith in Christ implies the existence of the Church in which Christ lives. And when St Leo again gives his voice to Peter he shows himself with his confession to be the living rock; he lets us know that the Church is founded on the rock of Peter; and he shows us this threefold aspect: the primacy of the love of Christ, concretized in the life of the living Church, and again concretized in the Petrine mystery, and in the succession of Peter who remains always present in his successors.

So we are led back through St Leo the Great to Mother Julia and to that which she began, to this new fidelity to Christ in His Church. When the "Holy Covenant" is at the centre of The Work, it is again nothing new next to Christ. It is an entering into the New Covenant which he gave; in the Covenant which is based on the gift of the Holy Eucharist; in the Covenant which comes from the Sacred Heart of Jesus, from which blood and water, the holy sacraments, flow. Her primacy of Christology, her love for Christ, expressed itself in the love for the pierced Heart of Jesus. It is not by chance, I think, that The Work considers itself a friend of Newman, with his motto *"Cor ad cor loquitur"*. Mother Julia thought from the heart and knew the Heart of Jesus – this pierced Heart, which is the source of the Covenant, the source of our life – from the heart.

When the symbol of the crown of thorns is added, it becomes evident that union with Christ means union with His suffering. That means, being ready to accept the wounds of the truth. Whoever stands up for the truth in a world in which lies are more comfortable accepts being wounded. And whoever stands up for love in this world, against egotism, which is nearer mankind, lets himself be wounded, says yes to the pierced Heart, says yes to the crown of thorns. This crown is the true king's crown, with which Christ proves Himself to be the true Lord of the world and shows us the face of the living God, who is Love and Forgiveness unto death. Through union with the suffering Christ we find ourselves in the midst of the afflictions of the times to be also in union with His glory, the glory which is love: Love is stronger than suffering, stronger than death.

The papal approbation is not a juridical formality for the Spiritual Family The Work. It is rather an expression of what The Work is, the confirmation of its deepest being in the Church, which is at the same time unity with Christ. When we thus grasp the gift of The Work and let it lead us into the Mystery of the Church, to find the Heart of Jesus and to let our hearts be enlightened by His, then we will have the same experience as Mother Julia: she knew and experienced that the seemingly heavy yoke of Christ is light because He carries it for us and with us, that his burden is good, because it is the burden of love. Let us pray that He may help us ever more deeply to experience this and to enter into the Work of Christ and thus to serve the salvation of the world. Amen.

Foreword

God never ceases to raise up men and women, endowed with special graces, 'living witnesses of his unchanging love'. They inspire us by their admirable lives. They attract others to share in the charism they received for the good of the entire community of the Church. They are shining stars in a world of darkness and error. The story of their lives and work is a fascinating one. The good they did lives on after them and is sustained by those who follow their example and are trained in the spirit that guided them.

The life of Julia Magdalena Verhaeghe or, as she became known by all her followers, Mother Julia or simply "Mother", spanned the greater part of the twentieth century. She was an outstanding woman of her time, known by a relatively small number of people, but deeply revered and venerated by those who came into closer contact with her work and spirit. The more she shunned the limelight, the higher the esteem others had for her. The penetrating insights she had into human frailty, her words of advice on how to advance on the journey of prayer, adoration and conversion, her love for Jesus and for the Church, made her a mistress of the spiritual life for many souls.

This first biography will reveal to many the story of Mother Julia's life and the wisdom of her teaching. It deals only with the first half of her life, but it has the value of situating it in the historical context in which she was born, grew up and received special graces. This background helps us to understand the points that are given particular emphasis in her charism: in a world of division and enmity, the grace of unity; in an era of declining faith, her insistence on the three sustaining pillars of faith, hope and love; in decades of error and confusion, her piercing understanding of the signs of the times in the light of the Gospel; in years when the Church sought to open up for the faithful the hidden treasures of the Letters of St Paul together with her insistence on a prayerful and dignified liturgical celebration and on the value of adoration; in the years when Bl. Edward Poppe's Eucharistic crusades touched the heart of the young in Belgium and St Therese of Lisieux was beatified, we understand better Mother Julia's love for the Eucharist and her insistence on God's merciful and just love.

Numerous people have waited for this book. It is an answer to their spontaneous request to be given more of the spiritual treasures that Mother Julia had received in abundance. The wisdom and approved way to holiness, enshrined in a charism, is meant for the good of all. Mother Julia herself would have wished it so, not for her own glorification, but for the Church and for individual souls.

I congratulate and thank all who have worked assiduously on the production of this biography. It will undoubtedly be of benefit to many, and will help to make known a recent charism of consecrated life, which was given by the Lord as an answer to the challenging times in which we live.

Philip Boyce, OCD
(Bishop of Raphoe, Ireland)

16 July 2005

Introduction

For the first time in the history of our Spiritual Family we present a publication on Julia Verhaeghe (1910-1997), the foundress of The Work, whom we gratefully call Mother. She was a woman of faith, full of wisdom, humble and modest. She wanted to serve God and her neighbour with all the gifts and graces God had given her. An unassuming person, quiet about herself, she shunned the limelight and asked expressly that no biography of her should be published in her lifetime. She spoke much about God, the Church and The Work, about the development of the People of God and of society, as also about the concrete events of daily life. She spoke of herself only when describing the ways God worked in her life. Two maxims marked her whole being which later became the two mottos of our Spiritual Family: *Ad laudem et gloriam Dei* – "For God's honour and glory" and *Ut omnes unum sint* –"That all may be one". These are the two pillars on which rest the charism of The Work, adoration and unity.

It never occurred to Mother Julia to found a Work. The circumstances of her life would have made it humanly impossible, as she did not have good health, had only received an elementary education, nor had she any financial means. Yet the Lord enkindled in her a vibrant faith, a burning love for the Church, and the ardent desire and readiness to offer herself and her life for the inner renewal of the Church. Thus she became the instrument which God used to create a new community in the Church: The Spiritual Family The Work.

It was her will, expressed in writing, that any presentation of her life would avoid anything which *'might distract the reader from the essential'* [1]. For her, the essential was the charism of The Work, the gift and grace, which the Lord bestowed on our Spiritual Family through her. This book gives an insight into her life, which cannot be separated from the charism of The

---

[1] See Mother Julia's notes from 19 March 1991. These and all the following unpublished sources without any further reference are kept in the private archives of the Spiritual Family The Work in the Convent of Thalbach in Bregenz, Austria.

Work. "*The charism is my biography*"[22], she declared in a conversation not long before her death. Throughout her life our Mother took her spiritual nourishment from Sacred Scripture, especially from the Letters of St Paul; her thinking was fully inspired by his. Drawing on insights she received when meeting people, from experiences in the liturgy or in daily life, she unfolded the principles of the charism and enabled others to discover the beauty of the Catholic faith.

We have kept faithfully to the documents concerning Mother Julia and Fr Arthur Cyriel Hillewaere, her spiritual director, which are kept in our archives, quoting only those words that are supported by written evidence. Often we let Mother Julia speak to the reader for herself. The photographs and maps are there to illustrate the text and to help our understanding of the events that are described. We will have to leave it to scholars in the future to add to these pages the fruit of their study of historical sources which are not yet available and from which a fuller view of the beginnings of The Work may emerge.

Every charism is a response by God to the existing difficulties and needs of the Church and of the world. To portray Mother Julia's life faithfully and to delineate accurately the development of the charism granted to her, it has been necessary to refer to the history of her birthplace, Geluwe, and to look at the Church and the social and political situation in Belgium at the time. It is only against this back-drop that we can understand details of our Mother's life and their importance for later developments.

Mother Julia wished that the vocation of The Work should always be seen in the context of the signs of the times, i. e. against the background of the respective historical situation and what arises from it, be it positive or negative. This book shows that Mother Julia's life and the beginnings of The Work were overshadowed by the horrors of the two World Wars and that they were linked to the development of Catholic Action, in particular to that of the Young Catholic Workers, a movement founded by Josef Cardijn, later Cardinal, which was extremely influential in Belgium.

During the last century society underwent a radical change of mentality. A distinctive mark of that transformation was the search for unity and for integration in all areas of life. As a result of the progress of modern

---

[2] Conversation with Mother Julia on 30 December 1995.

technology, the world has become more and more a global village, where everyone can communicate with everybody else. Politics and commerce have assumed new and worldwide dimensions. Different cultures have been enabled to engage with one another as never before. This process of globalisation has brought huge challenges but also many new opportunities for the Church. The charism of The Work has to be seen against the background of this new situation as it has different characteristics which urge in a Christian way to wholeness, integration, comprehensiveness, and universality.

It seemed appropriate to describe the beginnings of our Spiritual Family up to the year 1950. At that time the charism had reached an important stage in its development, and for the first time the Eucharistic Lord found a home in a house of The Work. The later development and growth of our family stretches into the present time. To bridge the gap between the past and the present a short survey of the development of The Work after 1950 up to its Pontifical recognition is added as an Appendix.

The recognition of The Work in the universal Church by the successor of St Peter took place on 29 August 2001, the fourth anniversary of Mother Julia's death. On our pilgrimage of thanksgiving to Rome we had the privilege of meeting Pope John Paul II on 10 November 2001. The Decree of the Pontifical recognition and also an address and message to our Spiritual Family by the late Holy Father can be found in the Appendix. The sermon which Joseph Cardinal Ratzinger – now Pope Benedict XVI – preached at the Mass of Thanksgiving in St Peter's Basilica is printed at the beginning of this volume. The Appendix contains a homily by Bishop Boyce, who for many years was Mother Julia's spiritual director, together with some extracts from a testimony by Leo Cardinal Scheffcyzk. An overview listing some important dates in the life of our Mother concludes the volume.

In this publication we hope to convey to the reader something of the grace-filled work of God in his Church – through the person of Mother Julia. We hope that this book enables the reader to come closer to the mystery of one who was truly a daughter of the Church and who lived a life that was marked by a noble simplicity, by love and truth. She lived for the Church, she suffered for the Church, and she offered herself as a sacrifice for the Church. She wrote: "*I am inwardly urged to express my deep joy and profound gratitude to the Church, my beloved Mother, though I do not know how to find the words. It is Christ's foundation to which I belong. It pleased God to choose me as an instrument of his merciful and just love for his Bride, the Church, who is marked by the sufferings of Christ. He wanted to grant to her a charism to help her in all her needs, a charism, for which He himself wants to be the plan and the guide, for He has promised to remain with his Church until everything is accomplished.*"[3]

As those with international responsibility for the Priests' Community and for the Sisters' Community of The Work, we would like to thank our brothers and sisters and all those who have helped with the composition of this book and with the necessary historical research. It could only have been written thanks to our close co-operation in love and in joint responsibility for the charism. We will be pleased if many are graced thereby with a personal, trusting relationship with Mother Julia.

MOTHER KATHARINA STROLZ, FSO   FR PETER WILLI, FSO, RECTOR

29 August 2005,
8th anniversary of Mother Julia's death

---

[3] Notes by Mother Julia from 20 May 1993.

FIRST PART

The years of childhood and youth
(1910-1934)

I. Early childhood

Where God is concerned nothing happens by chance. The great events of world history and the smallest occurrences of daily life conform to a mysterious plan, in which He is leading creation to its fulfilment. For those who are alert to the workings of divine providence, it is no accident that Julia was born on a Friday and baptised on a Sunday. Right from the start her life was illuminated by the mystery of the Lord's Passion and Resurrection.

Julia was born in the village of Geluwe in Belgium on Friday, 11 November 1910, at 11.00 in the morning. She was the eighth of eleven children, three boys and eight girls. Three of her siblings died in infancy, which was not uncommon at that time, as infant mortality was high.[1] On the following Sunday, 13 November, she was baptised in the parish church of her home village. This sacrament was to mark her entire life and to make her ever grateful.

The parish church of Geluwe in 1910

Julia's childhood was spent within the secure environment of a Christian family. Later in life she would sometimes reflect on that period: *"Whenever I speak of it, I do so, that you may know how wonderfully, how naturally and at the same time supernaturally God was with me, preparing me for the charism of the Work – through my parents and through my development as a child and adolescent."*[2]

Julia's parents came from Geluwe in West Flanders. Her father, Henry Verhaeghe, was a peace-loving man. He was both friendly and sensitive

---

[1] Cf. E. Huys, *Geschiedenis van Geluwe*, met aanvullingen door D. Decuypere, Geluwe: privately printed by Luc Demeester ³1977, p. 423. D. Decuypere, *Dorp zonder grenzen. 1940-1945 - epicentrum Geluwe*, Geluwe: privately printed 1985, p. 27.
[2] Conversation with Mother Julia, 22 February 1996.

Entry in the baptismal register of the parish in Geluwe

to the needs of others and found it easy to get on with people. He would gladly offer assistance if he saw someone in need. Before the First World War, he had worked in the paper and flax industries. In the area around Geluwe at that time there were large flax and tobacco fields, providing a living for numerous families. Henry even owned his own piece of land, on which he grew flax. Julia remembered: *"My father was an ordinary Christian, faithful, big-hearted, and completely dedicated to his family and children. He was a devoted and cheerful family man. God placed much wisdom in his words. He was highly regarded by everyone who knew him."* [3]

Julia's mother, Valentine Rosé, was a strong personality, who could be very kind and strict at the same time. Julia recalled: *"In spite of their different personalities, my father and mother complemented each other well in the upbringing of their children. My mother was a deeply religious woman. She was a good and wise teacher, a woman of Christian maturity, in a way that was rather unusual in a period so strongly marked by tradition. I was not an easy child to bring up. My mother often did not know how to take, or make sense of, what I said or kept to myself, since my words and my behaviour did not always correspond to what a child of my age was expected to hear, see or say."* [4]

An able housewife, Julia's mother cared lovingly for the well being of her husband and children, in spite of her poor health. She ensured that daily life was conducted with the minimum of fuss and with respect for others, refusing to permit superficial and pointless talk. She went about her work in the house carefully and conscientiously. After her day's work was done, in order to help her husband support their large family,

---

[3] Mother Julia's Notes, 1985.
[4] Mother Julia's Notes, 1990. Conversation with Mother Julia, 22 February 1996.

she would sometimes produce bobbin work late into the night by the dim light of an oil lamp. Henry lovingly supported her, assisting in the running of the household as far as his job would allow, baking bread and caring for the children.

The Catholic faith permeated every aspect of the Verhaeghe family's daily life, which was underpinned by prayer, holy Mass and the cultivation of the Christian virtues. They would frequently pray the rosary together and renew their consecration to the Sacred Heart. It was the parents' custom to bless the children reverently at bed-time.[5] The family liked to go on pilgrimage to Dadizele, the most important Marian shrine in West Flanders, which had been a place of pilgrimage since the fourteenth century.[6] Julia was very fond of this shrine. Years later, she wrote: *"It was a much loved place of grace for me. The church in Dadizele is a gem."* [7] She would go there with her family and other people from the parish every year on the 8 September, the feast of Our Lady's birth.

The basilica of Dadizele

Although Julia grew up in an environment marked by tradition, she soon revealed a particular spiritual gift, by which she was able to discern what was genuine and what was not in traditional ideas. In later years, she wrote: *"As a child, if I heard talk of religious matters or people that did not sound right to me, I would often think to myself: 'God is not like that'!"* [8]

From very early on, Julia developed a love for singing. Remi Ghesquiere, a native of Geluwe, was a well-known composer of hymns and a patron of Flemish folk music, who turned Geluwe into a village of song. Many of his songs, which Julia sang with joy and enthusiasm, were to accompany

---

[5] Cf. P. Boyce, *The Blessing*, Bregenz: privately printed, The Spiritual Family The Work 1981, p. 4.

[6] Cf. S. Desodt, *Geen rijker kroon dan eigen schoon. Onze Lieve Vrouw van Dadizele*, Dadizele: privately printed, no date.

[7] Mother Julia's Notes, 1985.

[8] Conversation with Mother Julia, written down 26 January 2004.

her throughout her life.[9]

In 1914 the First World War broke out. One of the causes of this terrible war was the growth of nationalism, which had been on the increase since the French revolution (1789).[10] As a consequence of this development, the individual nations began to view one another as opponents. At the same time, the military strength of some of these nations grew as a result of general conscription to the armed services, creating the conditions for war on a far larger scale than hitherto.

The decisive event leading to the outbreak of the First World War (1914-1918) occurred on 28 June 1914, when the heir to the Austro-Hungarian throne, Franz Ferdinand, was assassinated by Serbian nationalists in Sarajevo. On 23 July 1914, Austria issued a set of demands to Serbia (the July Ultimatum). Serbia rejected one of the demands, the involvement of Austria in the legal process against those involved in the plot. So, on 28 July, Austria with the support of Germany declared war on Serbia.[11] This was followed, on 1 August, by Germany's declaration of war on Russia, which was allied with France. Thus, at the beginning of the First World War, two power blocks faced each other. On one side stood the 'Central Powers', led by Germany and Austria and Italy, and, on the other side, the 'Allies', led by France, Russia and Great Britain. Because Germany had enemies in both the East and the West, she was threatened by war on two fronts.[12] For this reason she sought to defeat France as quickly as possible. In order to achieve this objective and to attack France from both North and East, German troops needed to be able to pass through Belgium.

On 3 August the German Kaiser, Wilhelm II, declared war on France, issuing Belgium with a twelve hour ultimatum, in which he said that Germany would regard Belgium as her enemy should the Belgians confront and offer resistance to German troops. The Belgian government rejected this ultimatum, since it threatened Belgium's neutrality. The next day, 4 August, German troops marched into Belgium.[13] On the same day,

---

[9] Cf. D. Decuypere, *Geluwnaren van taal en gemoed. Aspecten van een eeuw Vlaams denken op of vanuit Geluwe. 50 jaar Davidsfonds op Geluwe (1931-1981)*, Geluwe: Davidsfonds 1981, pp. 27-28.

[10] Cf. R. Aubert, *Der Ausbruch des 1. Weltkriegs*, in: Handbuch der Kirchengeschichte, Band VI/2: Die Kirche zwischen Anpassung und Widerstand, 1878 bis 1914, ed. H. Jedin, Freiburg-Basel-Wien: Herder 1973, pp. 538-545.

[11] Cf. A. Scheucher, A. Wald, H. Lein and E. Staudinger, *Zeitbilder, Geschichte und Sozialkunde*, Vol. 7: *Vom Beginn des Industriezeitalters bis zum Zweiten Weltkrieg*, Wien: öbv & hpt ²1999, pp. 70-71.

[12] Cf. A. Palmer and H. Thomas, *Die Moderne Welt im Aufbruch*, Meilensteine der Geschichte, Vol. III, translated by S. Erbe, S. De Gasperi, S. Hammer, u.a., Frankfurt-Berlin: Ullstein 1972, p. 185.

[13] Cf. N. Fischer, *Chronik 1914. Tag für Tag in Wort und Bild*, Die Chronik-Bibliothek des 20. Jahrhunderts, Vol. 14, ed. B. Harenberg, Dortmund, Chronik-Verlag ²1989, p. 126.

The Verhaeghe family during world war one from left to right: Madeleine; Henri, the father; Camille; Joseph; Adrienne; Augusta; Emma Valentine, the mother; Julia. Marie, the eldest daughter was in France

Great Britain declared war on Germany, because she had violated Belgian neutrality.

The number of countries involved in the war increased on both sides, with a total of ten million armed men confronting each other.[14] Within

German troops enter Geluwe

the first few weeks of the war, it was apparent that an era had ended.[15] The world order had changed forever.

In Belgium the invasion by German forces caused a huge flood of refugees. After the fall of Antwerp in October 1914 more than a million Belgians fled into Holland. In subsequent years, more than 250,000 people fled to Great Britain, and over 300,000 to France.[16]

Geluwe, which at that time had about 5,000 residents, became a battlefield on the Western Front. In a book about the history of the village, it says: *"The inhabitants of Geluwe watched in great fear as the battle front approached. Geluwe lay on the main road between Menin and Ypres, two cities, fortified since olden times, and so often fought over. Would it soon become a battleground too? Around 5 October, large contingents of German cavalry massed around the French town of Lille, and reached the border within a short space of time. On the same day German cavalry was seen at the bridge in Wervik. The whole town was in panic and fled to nearby Geluwe. While our streets were overflowing with refugees, a reconnaissance patrol rode through the village. On 6 October, after dark, 700 German cavalrymen swarmed into*

---

[14] Cf. A. Scheucher, A. Wald, H. Lein and E. Staudinger, *Zeitbilder*, p. 72.

[15] Cf. A. Palmer and H. Thomas, *Die Moderne Welt im Aufbruch*, p. 186.

[16] Cf. D. Decuypere, *Het malheur von de keizer. Geluwe 1914-1918*, Geluwe: printed privately 1998, p. 389.

the centre of the village and took possession of it. There are no words to describe how terrified the population was at this first, night-time occupation." [17]

In October 1914, during the first battle of Ypres, fifty men from Geluwe, who had not been called up into the army, were forced to collect the corpses of dead soldiers from the front and to throw them into mass graves. It was not only the trench warfare that produced innumerable casualties. Many soldiers died as a result of disease and exhaustion. According to *The History of Geluwe*: *"The ground was littered with the corpses of soldiers and slaughtered cattle. Among them were also the bodies of people from the village: the family of Jules Deprez – the father, the mother and the three children."* [18]

Julia's father also had to participate in this task, which was so terrible that some were unable to do it for long. It caused him and his family much suffering. When collecting the bodies of the dead, he would often have the painful thought: *"A father! A son! What sorrow for those who are left behind!"* [19] Julia still spoke of this in her old age: *"My father was also called on to do this work. I no longer remember for how long he was obliged to help in collecting the corpses. It made my father ill. He did not put up with this terrible work for very long."* [20]

After the occupation a local commandant was put in charge of Geluwe, taking over the offices of both the mayor and the chief of police.[21] The local population's freedom of movement was severely restricted. Even to enter an adjoining neighbourhood within the village one had to obtain a pass from the German occupiers. Heavy fighting would frequently break out. Sometimes the parish church was used as a hospital for wounded soldiers. At the end of October, about 200 injured British prisoners of war were brought there.[22]

The Verhaeghe family did not live in the centre of Geluwe, but to the west, on a large plot of land in Green Street between two farms. This area was declared prohibited and fenced off with barbed wire. Julia later told of how German troops were stationed in the large fields on either side of her parents' house: *"We children had to have a pass to cross to the other side of the street. You can imagine how concerned our parents were about*

---

[17] E. Huys, *Geschiedenis van Geluwe*, pp. 168f.
[18] *Ibid.*, p. 189.
[19] Conversation with Mother Julia, 25 May 1997.
[20] Conversation with Mother Julia, 19 October 1993.
[21] Cf. D. Decuypere, *Het malheur van de keizer*, p. 192.
[22] Cf. *ibid.*, pp. 77, 108 and 193.

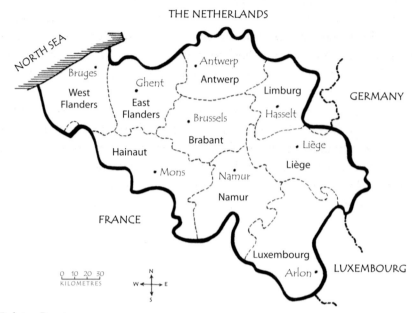

The Belgian Provinces

Important places in the life of Mother Julia

this, how fearful they became on account of us children, because we liked to play and just could not keep to these boundaries." [23] Julia would often cross over the boundary, because one of the German soldiers occasionally gave her chocolate. The family had to provide accommodation for one of the officers, who sometimes showed his gratitude by providing them with food.

Soon their neighbours began to take flight from this dangerous environment. The Verhaeghe family too considered fleeing to France with one of their uncles. However, Julia's mother was expecting her eleventh child and was very weak and ill. Little Bernadette died three weeks after her birth. The pain of this event left deep marks on Julia. In spite of the war, her parents felt obliged to remain in Geluwe for the time being.

---

[23] Mother Julia's Notes, 1985.

II. Fleeing from home in time of war

On 6 April 1917, the United States of America entered the war on the side of the Allies, following Germany's resumption of its unrestricted U-boat campaign, which threatened US merchant shipping bringing armaments and food supplies to the allied countries, and the discovery of Germany's attempt to form an alliance with Mexico and Japan against the USA. For Great Britain, France and Russia, the entry of the USA into the war marked a decisive strengthening of their military power.[1]

In the following months, the armed conflict on the Western Front in Belgium became even more intense. For those inhabitants of Geluwe, who had not yet fled, the situation became ever more life-threatening. The phased evacuation of Geluwe began, and more than a thousand inhabitants were ordered to leave the village.[2] *"On 7 June 1917, the sky became suddenly bright. Powerful explosions caused the earth to shake and tremble. Combat aircraft criss-crossed the skies. The preparations for the evacuation began."*[3]

On 5 October, in order to save the remaining inhabitants of the village from certain death, the local commandant gave the order for the total evacuation of Geluwe.[4] Together with many other villagers the Verhaeghe family were ordered to leave the village within a few hours, although their mother was weak and in poor health and their father too was ill. On 10 October, the soldiers led them away on a cart belonging to a neighbouring farm. They had no idea where they were going. Seven of the children went with them on the journey. (Marie, the oldest daughter, was working in a household in France.) They could only take the most basic necessities with them. Not long after they had set off, their father realised that, in the confusion of their departure, he had left behind a watch, a valuable and handsome family heirloom. The soldiers permitted him to turn back in order to rescue it. But returning to the family home, he was terribly shocked to see that it was already in flames. Little Julia

---

[1] Cf. S. REINHARDT, *Chronik 1917. Tag für Tag in Wort und Bild*, Die Chronik-Bibliothek des 20. Jahrhunderts, Vol. 17, ed. B. Harenberg, Dortmund, Chronik-Verlag ³1991, p. 65.

[2] Cf. E. HUYS, *Geschiedenis van Geluwe*, pp. 214-215.

[3] *Ibid.*, pp. 212-213.

[4] Cf. D. DECUYPERE, *Het malheur van de keizer*, p. 368; E. HUYS, *Geschiedenis van Geluwe*, pp. 211-221.

never forgot the expression of pain on the faces of her parents at the destruction of their house.

In the neighbouring town of Menin the refugees from Geluwe experienced once more the terror of bombardment. A bomb fell on a large building close to where they were staying.[5] The explosion was so great that the refugees were buried under tables, chairs and debris. As a result, on 12 October, some of them, including Julia with her parents and siblings, were taken in cattle trucks to Lembeek near Halle.[6] There they found shelter in a house belonging to the Brothers of the Christian Schools (De La Salle Brothers),[7] who took in people from many different places and showed great consideration for the needs of the refugees. The dispossessed were a mixture of good and bad. The influence of the latter was the source of real concern to the Verhaeghe parents, who were worried at the potentially dangerous effect on the upbringing of their children. So they were very thankful, when they were eventually able to move into a small house in Lembeek, where they could lead a normal family life.

Augusta, Julia's sister, said of this difficult time: *"At first we had neither tables nor chairs. We just sat on the floor in the straw, until the mayor provided us with a table, chairs and an oven. We also received blankets, which we later made into clothes for us girls. Thank God that there were good people, who helped us."* [8] Nevertheless, the refugee children were frequently hungry, because food was so hard to come by. Julia remarked shortly before her death: *"In our earliest childhood we had two or three years without any normal meals."*[9]

It was in these difficult circumstances that the young Julia became acquainted with life's hardships. She spent two and a half years as a refugee child with her family in Lembeek. She remembered fondly the generosity and helpfulness of some of the inhabitants of the village. However, she experienced a spiritual coldness pervading the atmosphere of this industrial community. It was here that she confronted for the first time the alienation from the faith that had infiltrated many industrial areas. From her room overlooking the nearby cemetery she repeatedly

---

[5] Cf. D. Decuypere, *Het malheur van de keizer*, p. 369.

[6] Cf. *ibid.*, p. 370; J. Durnez, *Over 't Roosetje en zijn bewoners* …, Geluwe: printed privately 1983, p. 26; Frères Des Ecoles Chrétiennes, Archives de la Maison Généralice, Rome EA 133/2 dos. 5.

[7] Cf. Menen Town Archives, Evacuation du 12 October 1917 sur Halle: Waalvest z/n (Archive box with refugee list).

[8] Conversation with Mrs Augusta Overbergh-Verhaeghe (1907-2002), 18 May 2000.

[9] Conversation with Mother Julia, 25 May 1997.

In this group of refugees from Geluwe and Menin is the Verhaeghe family. In the oval is Julia

The refugees were sent to this house of the Brothers of the Christian Schools

Excerpt of list of refugees who arrived at Lembeek on 12 October 1917

witnessed the burials of dead workers without the presence of a priest. She was distressed by such events and could not understand how they should be allowed to happen. In later years she was conscious that even in her childhood she had been acutely aware of behaviour that conflicted with the faith.

In order to earn the family's daily bread, Julia's father sought work in a factory. He was forced to face the fact that a freethinking and unbelieving mentality had spread amongst parts of the workforce. This mentality, which he had rarely encountered before, weighed heavily on him. After a short period, with the help of providence, he found a more amenable position in the presbytery of Lembeek. Two of his daughters, Augusta and Marie, were already employed there; Marie having returned from France. The Verhaeghe family were always very thankful to the priests for providing them with work. They were sometimes able to obtain food from the presbytery to alleviate some of the privation within their own household. The poor health of Julia's mother was a constant worry for her father and the children. On several occasions she was so close to death that she received the last rites. At this time, the family received a great deal of support from Doctor Spitaels, Lembeek's mayor and doctor, who cared attentively for their sick mother.

The parish church of Lembeek

Julia went for the first time to Confession and Holy Communion in the parish church of Lembeek. Unexpected circumstances overshadowed these events. Because of illness, Julia could not make her first Confession and first Holy Communion with the other children, but had to do so somewhat later. She made her first Confession as her classmates went to Confession for the second time. The little Julia was excited and nervous. The priest did not know that this was her first confession and interrupted her, because he could not fully understand her West Flemish dialect. He then used a word for a refugee child that had derogatory connotations in her dialect.[10] Julia left the confessional in tears without waiting for absolution. The class teacher, a nun, was supervising the children in the church and noticed what had happened. She mentioned it to another priest who would understand Julia's dialect better, and, with fatherly concern, he heard her confession in the sacristy. Her first reception of the Sacrament of Penance and her first Holy Communion made a deep impression on Julia's young soul. A profound love of Jesus was already growing within her.

On occasion she was allowed to accompany her father on pilgrimage from Lembeek to Halle. Together they would visit the beautiful basilica in the town. What particularly impressed Julia there was the life-sized statue of Christ, bound and crowned with thorns, on the exterior of the church: *"Each time my young mind was touched by the terrible sufferings that Christ had taken on himself."* [11]

In Lembeek, on 12 July 1919, she was an eyewitness with her father to a fatal train crash. It happened as she waited in front of the barrier of a level crossing. Whenever she spoke of it later she had the impression of seeing the event again like a film: the victims gushing with blood, the limbs, the groans and screams of the injured survivors lying among the heaps of twisted iron, and the commotion amongst the bystanders. Her father jumped immediately into the train driver's cab and turned off the engine. Fourteen people lost their lives in this accident.[12]

Statue of Christ crowned with thorns outside the basilica of Halle

In spite of all the difficulties, Julia remembered the years in Lembeek with gratitude, as a time when she had felt secure in the heart of her family. Although compulsory education had only been introduced in Belgium in

---

[10] Cf. D. DECUYPERE, *Het malheur van de keizer*, pp. 403-405.

[11] Conversation with Mother Julia, written down 11 November 2000.

[12] Cf. *Hallensia. Bulletin van de Koninklijke Geschied- en Oudheidkundige Kring van Halle*, Nieuwe Reeks, 1 (April-June 1979/2) 12; ANON., 'La catastrophe de chemin de fer de Lembecq' in *L'Evénement Illustré*, 5 (17 July 1919/195) 379; LEMBEEK Community Archives, death register.

1914[13] and the law could not be enforced during the war years, Julia's parents were determined that she should attend a primary school, run by the Sisters of Christian Schools from Vorselaar. During the holidays Julia sometimes helped out in a house of the same community outside of Lembeek. The Sisters, faithful to the spirit of their congregation, were spiritual mothers to her, providing her with both affection and direction. She still remembered them many years later: *"They were so good to us!"* [14]

In the terrible years of the First World War, the Lord had begun to shape Julia's soul and to prepare it for a special mission. She said of this period: *"I was nurtured and formed in the poverty of Bethlehem in the midst of the chaos of war. God needs none of those things that the world needs in order to form a person. God knows what He gives and what He takes."* [15]

---

[13] Cf. D. DECUYPERE, *Geluwnaren van taal en gemoed*, p. 11.

[14] Conversation with Mother Julia, 10 May 1993.

[15] Conversation with Mother Julia, 23 May 1997.

III. Return and reconstruction

On 11 November 1918, Julia's eighth birthday, the First World War came to an end. In Belgium, more than 76,000 people had died – 23,000 civilians and 53,000 soldiers. Many had perished in the terrible battles at the front, whilst others were victims of illness, epidemics and the deprivations of war. The total loss of life in battle was between eight and nine million soldiers. Twenty one million were wounded, and six and a half million were held as prisoners of war. Untold numbers of civilians also lost their lives.[1]

There was much devastation in West Flanders. In the Diocese of Bruges, to which Geluwe belongs, 84 churches were destroyed and over 50 were damaged.[2] Geluwe lay in ruins with 869 houses completely destroyed. *"The village was an awful sight. In the village square only four of the houses had a roof. The Terhand area was just like a heap of intertwined, collapsed roofs, over which an undamaged Crucifix stretched out its reconciling*

Geluwe in 1918

arms. In the western end of the village there were no buildings left standing. On the Koelenberg one could count 8,000 grenade holes in a 35 hectare area."[3]

Because of its strategic importance on the Western Front, Geluwe was badly affected by the fierce battles that took place there. Leading politicians sought to bring about the reconstruction of the devastated village. Dirk Decuypere, one of the most knowledgeable people on the

[1] Cf. S. REINHARDT, *Chronik 1917. Tag für Tag in Wort und Bild*, Die Chronik-Bibliothek des 20. Jahrhunderts, Volume 18, ed. B. Harenberg, Dortmund, Chronik-Verlag ²1988, p. 186; H. FAELENS, *Front 14/18 - Langs de Ijzer - Parcours*, Brussels: Artis-Historia 1993, p. 32.
[2] Cf. M. CLOET (Ed.), *Het bisdom Brugge (1559-1984). Bisschoppen, priesters, gelovigen*, Bruges: privately printed, Westvlaams Verbond van kringen voor heemkunde ²1985, p. 439.
[3] Cf. E. HUYS, *Geschiedenis van Geluwe*, p. 228, cf. *ibid.*, pp. 235-237.

history of Geluwe, writes: *"Occasionally we received visits from important people, who wanted to see how things were for the inhabitants of Geluwe and the surrounding towns and villages. King Albert I and Queen Elizabeth, the Ministers Renquin and de Broqueville, and the American Consul honoured our village with their presence. Menin even received a visit from the American President, Woodrow Wilson."* [4]

From the spring of 1919 many huts were built in Geluwe as emergency accommodation for the returning refugees with the help of the King Albert Fund.[5] The Verhaeghe family was able to return to Geluwe in March 1920.[6] They were housed in an emergency shelter with a roof of steel sheets, which came from a British army camp. Rent had to be paid for the furniture as well as the accommodation. Each hut contained an oven, five chairs, two benches, a table, two curtains, a wardrobe, a bread bin, large and small beds with mattresses and two blankets per bed.[7] Julia later recalled: *"We lived in two huts near the railway station, because our family was very big – 10 people. It was poor, but clean, and furnished as comfortably as possible with the little that was available."* [8]

After their return the Verhaeghe family lived from 1920 to 1923 in two huts of this type

In the period after the homecoming, in which up to 90 per cent of the population were unemployed in some regions of Belgium,[9] Julia's father helped in the clean-up operation that was necessary as a result of the devastation caused by the war. In 1923 he was able to acquire a small house in the Moerput district of Geluwe with the assistance of the organisation, *'Eigener Herd'* (literally, 'One's Own Hearth'), which offered financial aid to returning refugees.[10] Julia spent the remainder of

[4] Cf. D. DECUYPERE, *Dorp zonder grenzen*, p. 10.

[5] Cf. *ibid.*, p. 8; E. HUYS, *Geschiedenis van Geluwe*, p. 229.

[6] Cf. GELUWE Community Archive, Register van Bevolking 09.03.1920: Book Nos. 6, 88.

[7] Cf. D. DECUYPERE, *Het malheur van de keizer*, pp. 494-495.

[8] Mother Julia's Notes, 1985.

[9] Cf. D. DE KEYZER, *"Madame est servie". Leven in Dienst van adel en burgerij (1900-1995)*, Leuven: Van Halewyck ⁵1996, p. 360.

[10] Attested by notary Dupont, Geluwe, 15 September 1923, cf. MINISTERIE VAN FINANCIEN, *Beheer der*

her childhood there. Her father found work in a paper mill in the town of Busbeke in France, which employed more than 800 people, half of whom commuted from Belgium. As an engineer he was responsible for the upkeep and maintenance of the machinery. He soon won the respect of both his managers and fellow-workers, as a result of the diligence he showed in his work. Although his health was poor, he walked to work every morning and in all weathers, the journey taking about an hour. The walk home in the evening took just as long. In this way he was able to earn a living for himself and his family in the difficult times after the war.

By now Julia was already taking an active interest in everything going on in her neighbourhood, sometimes surprising her parents with her observations and her powers of discrimination. Amidst all the privation she showed a real openness to new technology. The few, expensive bicycles in Geluwe excited her interest, particularly as one of her neighbours used to cycle to work. One Sunday at Mass the priest preached a sermon on the theme of 'progress' and warned against the dangers of cycling, without expanding on his reasons for doing so. When at lunch Julia's parents asked

In 1923 the Verhaeghe family moved to this house

the children what the sermon had been about, Julia was silent until someone mentioned bicycles: *"Yes, he preached that cycling is evil. But I don't see why it is evil to get somewhere quicker. I would so love to have a bicycle!"* [11]

In these years Julia got to know the *Eucharistic Children's Crusade* which was inspired by the 1914 Eucharistic Congress in Lourdes and later spread to many countries including Belgium.[12] This movement was one of the fruits of Pope Pius X's determination to promote both frequent communion and communion among children. It had as its aim the awakening in the hearts of children a love of the Eucharistic Lord and of

registratie en domeinen, Bestuur Brugge, Grondpandbewaring Yperen. Annwijzingregister der hypothecaire formalitateiten, 1923, No 75bis; No 27. Ministère Des Finances, *Administration de l'enregistrement et des Domaines*, Direction à Bruges, Conservation à Ypres, Registre de transcription 1921, Case 48.

[11] Conversation with Mother Julia, 10 December 1993.

[12] Cf. K. Hofmann, 'Eucharistischer Kinderkreuzzug' in J. Hofer and K. Rahner (Eds.), *Lexikon für Theologie und Kirche*, Vol. 3, Freiburg: Herder [2]1959, 1165.

the Blessed Virgin Mary and the development of a spirit of self-sacrifice through regular gatherings, catechesis and its own periodical.[13] One of the most important and influential figures of the *Eucharistic Crusade* in Belgium was Fr Edward Poppe (1890-1924), who was beatified by Pope John Paul II on 3 October 1999. Julia met this zealous servant of the Church when he visited her school, and he left an indelible mark on her soul: *"Fr Edward Poppe was an instrument of God in my childhood. He was the door, as it were, through which my soul opened itself to the light of the mystery of the Eucharist. Through the Eucharistic movement for children, I experienced a strong inner attraction to the Eucharistic Lord, who seized, led and nourished me by His holy presence."* [14]

The *Eucharistic Crusade* strengthened Julia in her love for Jesus and in her striving after virtue. It made a tremendous impression on her, as she was to testify nearly sixty years later: *"At the weekly meeting our consciences received a sound formation, in which above all the meaning of, and the love for, sacrifice and mortification were brought home to us. I remember how at one of the weekly gatherings I was seized by this love of sacrifice, which found expression in all manner of acts of self-denial and in concrete deeds. We were made to understand all this through simple examples."* [15]

Julia as at the age of 12

An inner longing to form her character through love and the overcoming of self was awakened in Julia. At home she took on those little chores which previously she had done unwillingly, such as the washing up, polishing the copper, and cleaning the oven: *"The effect was that after I got used to doing these chores I developed a real liking for such work. It was like a first conversion to a more ardent and*

---

[13] Cf. R. BOUDENS, *De Kerk in Vlaanderen*. Momentopnamen, Averbode-Apeldoorn: Altoria 1994, pp. 285-289.
[14] Mother Julia's Notes, 17 May 1986. Letter of Mother Julia, 21 March 1990.
[15] Mother Julia's Notes, August 1984.

intimate love of Jesus in the Holy Eucharist and to Mary, his Mother. And so I experienced a deep, inner growth, which influenced my later life and gave it direction." [16]

At the feast of Corpus Christi on 15 June 1922, Julia was allowed to receive the so-called 'solemn communion'. In this ceremony, which still takes place in Belgium today, young people of about twelve years of age publicly profess their faith and renew their baptismal vows. Doctor Morlion, a doctor in Geluwe, gave Julia the dress she wore for this special occasion. Julia's sister, Augusta, testified: *"Doctor Morlion always had a particular fondness for Julia. For the 'solemn communion' he provided her with a new outfit: a new dress, a lovely hat and other items."* [17]

What caused Doctor Morlion, an unassuming and religious man, to undertake this act of charity? He had been called to the Verhaeghe household when Julia was being born, as the midwife could not be contacted. This was the first time he had delivered a baby in Geluwe, and as a consequence he developed a special bond with the Verhaeghe family and with Julia in particular. This attachment involved not just a natural sympathy, but was based on the fact that he was attracted to a special religious disposition that he saw in the young Julia. So one day he asked her to pray for one of his sons, that he would become a priest. Julia commented later that from a very early age God had given her a love for vocations to the priesthood and the religious life: *"I had to undergo many*

Doctor Léon Morlion, physician in Geluwe

trials. I offered up in prayer this inner struggle, together with my petitions, to the fatherly and merciful goodness of God, trusting that He would grant my request. By this time I bore in my heart a great love for the Church, the priesthood and vocations. Later I heard with joy and thanksgiving that the Lord had heard my prayer and the second son had become a priest." [18]

In August 1922, Cyriel Arthur Hillewaere, a priest of the diocese of Bruges, was appointed curate to Geluwe. He had been born in Lichtervelde

---

[16] *Ibid.*

[17] Conversation with Mrs Augusta Overbergh-Verhaeghe, 22 August 2000.

[18] Mother Julia's Notes, 1985.

Fr Arthur Hillewaere in 1922

on 18 January 1888 and attended secondary schools in France and Belgium. After philosophy studies in Roeselare and theological studies in Bruges, he was ordained a priest on 1 June 1912. He had wanted to enter a community of priests, but the Bishop had not permitted him to do so. He taught Latin and Greek for ten years in a secondary school in Poperinge.[19] From 1922 to 1939 he was a curate in Geluwe. At that time it was quite normal, on account of the large number of vocations, for a priest to remain a curate for many years before becoming a Parish Priest.

As a zealous pastor and man of prayer, he soon won the trust of the people. One woman remarked: *"Fr Hillewaere was a simple man, who got on well with everybody and always had words of encouragement for them all. He used to cycle through the village. He knew everyone and would speak to anyone. He was a prayerful priest, who was often to be seen in Church, and at the same time he had a real social conscience. He was always content and happy."* [20] Fr Hillewaere was particularly concerned with the generation of young people, who had imbibed liberal ideas during the war and who were unsure in their faith. He tried to understand the signs of the times with foresight and the power of discernment and to be a good shepherd to the people. In later years, Julia wrote of him, *"He was a spiritual father to the generation which grew up in the confusion and disorder of the post-war years and which was so influenced by contact with new people and ideas, striving after a higher standard of living built solely on material prosperity and cultural and technological progress."* [21]

The new curate worked together with the Parish Priest, Fr Hector Deslypere, a wise and well-regarded pastor, to tackle their shared pastoral responsibilities. Along with the Head Teacher of the school, Mr.Vervaeke, and the Sisters of Saint Vincent de Paul, they supported the returning refugees in word and deed, encouraging them to trust that God would

[19] Cf. R. ORROI, *Archief College: Leerkrachten Lagere School - School voor aangepast onderwijs - Secundaire school 1657-2001*, Poperinge: Sint-Stanislas College 2001 (archief.college.poperinge@sip.be), *Alfabetische lijst leerkrachten*, p. 35
[20] Recollections of Mother Julia, written down 6 May 2002.
[21] Letter of Mother Julia, 1 May 1992.

provide them with a future.[22]

It was not long before the young Julia caught Fr Hillewaere's attention. He wrote: *"She was sensitive – a thoughtful, shy and quiet girl."* [23] God eventually led him to become her confessor and the nurturer of her spiritual development.

After her return from Lembeek Julia attended the elementary school run by the Sisters of Mercy. She liked going to this school and enjoyed learning and acquiring practical skills. Even at this stage she possessed a sense for discerning what was genuine and sincere in her fellow pupils and teachers. Of Sr Clara, one of her teachers, she wrote: *"She was a genuine religious - patient, devoted, even-handed and fair in her dealings with her pupils."* [24]

When Julia was fourteen years old, she was confronted by the repeatedly disingenuous behaviour of one of her teachers. Frustrated by this, she tried to avoid the teacher: *"I felt a strong aversion to her, and was obstinate and grudging in my attitude, thinking and behaviour towards her. I was very unhappy."* [25] Julia gave in to the temptation to withdraw from the company of others, retreating silently into herself. One day she recognised that this self-centred silence was not right. She realised that she had to change and undertake acts of virtue. So she tried to overcome this negative frame of mind by deliberately speaking to others and seeking out their company, as well as performing acts of charity, whenever the opportunity arose. Through this experience she increased in self-knowledge and came in time to grasp how weakness could determine human behaviour. As she grew up, she was able to forgive the teacher with whom she had had so many problems: *"I feel no resentment towards her. I pray to the God of compassion, that He will have mercy on us both."* [26]

On 8 July 1924, Julia received the Sacrament of Confirmation. The power of the Holy Spirit gave her the courage to face up to life's struggles and to seek a greater union with Jesus. It was at this time that she first felt a silent longing to give her life to God and to become a Sister. One of her teachers, Sister Emilie, had touched her soul profoundly: *"Sometimes I was allowed to be alone with her. In the holidays she taught me embroidery. I enjoyed that very much. Her whole being, consecrated to God, had a positive*

---

[22] Cf. H. DRIESSENS, 'Wij zijn samen oderweg…' in *Geluwe - Sint-Dionysius*, Weekblad, 50 (13 January 1972), 1.
[23] Fr Hillewaere's Notes from the years 1922-1924. Cf. also extracts of Father Hillewaere from Mother Julia's account of 1935. From now on quoted as: 'Extracts from Mother Julia's account, 1935'.
[24] Mother Julia's Notes, 24 August 1992.
[25] *Ibid.*
[26] Conversation with Mother Julia, written down 31 March 2002.

influence on me and awakened in me the silent longing to become a Sister consecrated to God one day." [27]

At the age of fourteen, Julia was inwardly moved by two events, which remained imprinted on her memory. On 17 May 1925, Thérèse of Lisieux was canonised. Julia, who had up to that point shown no particular interest in this saint, testified as follows many years later: *"In 1925, on the day of the canonisation of Thérèse of Lisieux, I experienced something for the first time in my young life: Saint Thérèse called me to follow the little way of faith and to trust in God's merciful love. She gave direction to my conscience, which had been oppressed and burdened by what I experienced within and around me. She brought me to devotion to the divine Heart, the source of all mercy."* [28] On 11 December of the same year, Pope Pius XI (1922-1939) published the Encyclical, *Quas Primas*, with which he established the celebration of Christ the King as a feast day for the universal Church. It was at that time that the foundations of Julia's love for Christ the King were laid in her soul. *"I still remember"*, Julia declared, *"what a deep impression these two events made on me, how they spoke to me, and how they penetrated my life."* [29]

Looking back on the First World War and the following years, Julia testified: *"These afflictions shaped my early life, my upbringing and my entire personal, religious, intellectual and spiritual development."* [30] Through such experiences, God began to prepare her for a mission that she would only come to grasp after many years: *"Only later in life, when the charism had taken concrete form in me, was I able to make sense of such childhood experiences in the light of God's plan for the silent growth of that charism in me – just as I was – with both the good and the not so good sides of my character. In my childhood I was no better than others, just different. Not everything in me was harmony and unity, but I was driven always and in everything to unity, to what was essential. This did not come from within me, but was given to me."* [31]

---

[27] Mother Julia's Notes, 24 August 1992.
[28] Mother Julia's Notes, 17 May 1986.
[29] Letter of Mother Julia, 6 June 1975.
[30] Letter of Mother Julia, 30 May 1991.
[31] Conversations with Mother Julia, 22 February 1996 and 12 July 1997.

IV. Encounter with the Apostle Paul

At the beginning of the twentieth century, the liturgical movement spread through many countries. The Congress of Catholic Associations, which took place in Mechelen in 1909, marked the beginnings of the movement in Belgium. Its goal was to place the Mass once more at the heart of Christian life. For hundreds of years the liturgy had been largely the province of the clergy. Although the people of God demonstrated a sincere involvement in the sacrifice of the Mass, showed reverence in the presence of the Lord in the Eucharist, and placed their trust in His grace, their ability to participate actively in the celebration of the Mass was severely limited. During the Mass the faithful would busy themselves with private devotions that frequently bore little relation to what was happening in the liturgy. The liturgical movement enriched the spiritual lives of many people. At the Mechelen Congress the Benedictine monk, Lambert Beauduin, proposed introducing the use of the missal as a prayer book, making it accessible to the faithful by translating the entire text of the Latin Mass and Sunday Vespers into the vernacular. He said: *"The liturgy is the true prayer of the faithful. It is a powerful bond of unity and a complete instruction in the faith."* [1]

Fr Hillewaere was keen to promote the liturgical movement. As a faithful pastor he wanted to give the young Julia's religious longings a positive direction and to provide the necessary spiritual nourishment to feed them. He knew that God's grace was at work in her, so he gave her a Latin-Dutch missal when she was fifteen or sixteen years old. This allowed her to have a better understanding of the readings and prayers of the Mass and to draw on the riches of Sacred Scripture and the liturgy with greater awareness. This missal played an important role in Julia's religious development and formation.

---

[1] F. KOLBE, 'Die liturgische Bewegung' in *Der Christ in der Welt. Eine Enzyklopädie*, Band IX/4, ed. J. Hirschmann, Aschaffenburg: Pattloch 1964, 33f. Cf. E. ISERLOH, 'Innerkirchliche Bewegungen und ihre Spiritualität' in *Handbuch der Kirchengeschichte*, Vol. VII: *Die Weltkirche im 20. Jahrhundert*, ed. H. Jedin und K. Repgen, Freiburg-Basel-Wien: Herder 1979, 303f.

The mass formular with the second letter of Saint Paul to Timothy in the Latin-Dutch missal of 1921

Approximately seventy years later Julia told of her experiences as a result of being given the missal, as if they had occurred the day before: *"At that time Sacred Scripture was not often available in the vernacular. For the first time I had a missal in which the readings and the Gospel were not only printed in Latin, but also in Dutch. I opened this treasure chest with great joy and love. It was as if a fire had been lit within me. I could not explain it. On the first evening I tried to meditate on the prayers, readings and Gospel, everything in fact that was going to be prayed or sung at holy Mass the next morning. The words of Sacred Scripture fascinated me. For us children and young people it was self-evident that we should go to Mass every day."* [2]

At this time Julia found herself in a difficult situation. Shortly before Fr Hillewaere had given her the missal, she had been asked to assist at a special dinner. Whilst serving at table, she heard a priest speak irreverently about matters of faith to the amusement of others. Julia was shocked by the fact that a priest should make fun of holy things. She felt wounded and troubled in the depths of her soul. Never before had she experienced so painfully human weakness within the Church.

New conflicts, particularly confrontation with the pride and the dishonesty of some people, contributed to an increasing inner paralysis: *"It all pushed me slowly into a kind of crisis of faith. I was totally unhappy, alone, withdrawn, and imprisoned in myself. I endeavoured to develop a genuine and pure relationship with God through silent sacrifices and a sincere striving after virtue. Nevertheless, I experienced a sort of alienation in the life of faith. A certain superficiality or passivity began to overwhelm me."* [3] The feeling of insecurity in her soul lingered, and her trust in the Church diminished. Because of the temptations pulling her in different directions, she no longer knew what to do and yearned for help. *"It was when I was in this state that God's merciful justice intervened in my life in the most simple*

---

[2] Conversations with Mother Julia, 10 December 1993 and 27 December 1994.
[3] Mother Julia's Notes, 20 May 1993.

and, for me, most wonderful and all-encompassing manner." [4]

One evening, not long after she had received the missal, Julia did her usual preparation for Mass, reading the next day's liturgical texts. Nothing particularly struck her in the readings, but the next day during the readings at Mass, she was suddenly gripped in the depths of her soul by the words of St Paul, and for a short while lost consciousness of her surroundings: *" 'For the time is coming when people will not endure sound teaching.' (2 Tim 4:3.) I was so seized by this declaration of St Paul, that I seemed to be totally immersed in the substance of the text.*

An inside view of the parish church in Geluwe, where Julia met interiorly St Paul

It seemed to me that Paul had revealed its deepest meaning to me and had invited me to order my life according to it." [5]

The words that had overwhelmed her come from the second letter to Timothy. They stand as the testament of the great apostle to his spiritual son:

"I charge you in the presence of God and of Christ Jesus who is to judge the living and the dead, and by his appearing and his kingdom: preach the word, be urgent in season and out of season, convince, rebuke, and exhort, be unfailing in patience and in teaching. For the time is coming when people will not endure sound teaching, but having itching ears they will accumulate for themselves teachers to suit their own likings, and will turn away from listening to the truth and wander into myths. As for you, always be steady, endure suffering, do the work of an evangelist, fulfil your ministry. For I am already on the point of being sacrificed; the time of my departure has come. I have fought the good fight, I have finished the race, I have

Julia at the age of 16

---

[4] *Ibid.*
[5] Conversation with Mother Julia, 10 December 1993. Mother Julia's Notes, August 1984.

kept the faith. Henceforth there is laid up for me the crown of righteousness, which the Lord, the righteous judge, will award to me on that Day, and not only to me but also to all who have loved his appearing." (2 Tim 4:1-8)

Towards the end of her life Julia testified: *"This text has been like a summons from God's providence to my whole life right up until today. It was the first seed of the charism of The Work."* [6]

At that time she experienced something of the imperishable nature of the Word of God. Holy Scripture, in which God's light shines forth in its supernatural glory, became a source of consolation, power, and joy to her. She wrote later that God's Word *"powerfully directs those who welcome it in faith, listen to this Word, and accept and obey it with an open heart."* [7] It was not on the evening that Julia had read the Pauline text in private that she was seized by it, but during the Eucharistic celebration the next day. In this way the liturgy, in which God's Word has its real place, took on a fundamental significance in Julia's life.

Thereafter, the Apostle Paul was Julia's teacher, leading her further and further into the riches of the faith and into the mystery of the Church. He helped her to obtain inner peace once more and to grow in her love for the Church: *"His letters provided me with a strength-giving and much loved nourishment. I discovered in them, if I may put it this way, the holy Church, and conceived a great love for the mystical body of Christ. I was, as it were, infused with this mystery, which has always accompanied me since. The Apostle Paul became for me an instrument of God, a spiritual leader and a beloved brother, whose presence I could come to know and experience. In those days, it was as if I went through a second conversion, towards the heart of Jesus and towards His body, the Church."* [8]

Paul had entered unexpectedly into the life of the young Julia. She found in him a friend, who formed her conscience. Little by little she underwent a change in her thinking, which gave her the strength to be open to the gifts of God's mercy. People who met her noticed that she had an inner strength. Her prayer became more contemplative. Someone, who often prayed in the parish church in Geluwe, testified: *"I normally went to Church every day in the morning. The first person I would notice there was a dignified young woman, who usually knelt close to the altar. Her whole demeanour radiated contemplation. She was, as it were, lost in prayer."* [9]

---

[6] Conversation with Mother Julia, 27 December 1994.
[7] Mother Julia's Notes, December 1993.
[8] Mother Julia's Notes, August 1984.
[9] Recollections of Mother Julia, written down 24 September 1997.

By degrees Paul opened her eyes to the decline in faith, which was spreading like a dark cloud announcing a thunderstorm. She felt that the Apostle wanted to provide her with direction and help in responding to the needs of the times. The great religious poverty, the collapse of morals, the increasing rejection of the Church, the weaknesses within the people of God, as well as the progressive secularisation of all areas of life, threatened to lead to a modern heathenism.[10] Paul helped Julia to understand that conversion and faith provide the strength to remain loyal in the midst of new trials: *"This beloved brother and father showed me the path of profound conversion and led me in the spirit of discernment."* [11]

Julia preserved the light of grace she received from the Apostle Paul like a precious treasure in her heart, even in times of spiritual searching and struggle. Towards the end of her life she wrote: *"I am very conscious of the fact that Saint Paul, who taught me the Word of God, was the instrument of grace in my life. He helped to open my eyes to the grace and the kindness of the merciful love of God, which had been hidden in the golden threads that ran through my life. He had given me a key, which opened my heart to the divine commands and laws. Thus I was able to understand that the works of God obey supernatural laws, which often cut against the grain of human considerations; that the Word of God, when it is received with an open heart, contains an amazing, transforming power; that our life's merits and their supernatural effects are not dependent on the level of our activity, but on the love which animates us and which is poured into our soul through the Holy Spirit. For it is love that makes it possible for us to see God in everybody and everything."* [12]

---

[10] Cf. L. Vos, P. Wynants and A. Tihon, 'De christelijke arbeidersjeugd' in E. Gerard (Ed.), *De christelijke arbeidersbeweging in België* (Kadoc-Studies 11), Leuven: Universitaire Pers 1991, pp. 413-479.

[11] Letter of Mother Julia, 24 February 1987.

[12] Letter of Mother Julia, 4 February 1983.

V. New experiences in the world

In Belgium in the first half of the twentieth century hundreds of thousands of young women had to go into domestic service and to contribute to the upkeep of their families.[1] As a rule there were no written contracts, only verbal agreements. The young women were therefore very dependent on the good will of their employers.[2] Consequently, some were exploited, whilst others were treated as members of the family.

Julia belonged to that generation for whom there was no easy passage from childhood to adulthood, the years of childhood often being followed immediately by entry into the world of hard work.[3] In spite of her many talents she could no longer continue at school, but worked as a nanny and as a domestic maid in various families mainly in France, but also in Belgium.

In the same years that the Apostle Paul entered into her life, a new world, previously little known to her, opened up before Julia. She wrote later to Fr Hillewaere: *"I had to take up employment at an early age, without knowledge of the evil and dangers of the world. I can't express in words how much I suffered from this sudden change in my circumstances. It was no longer possible for me to attend Mass and go to Communion every day. My visits to Jesus in the Church had to be less frequent, just when I needed Him even more. But one idea gave me courage: 'Soon I will be grown up and will be able to enter a convent. Everything that I learn now, I will surely be able to use later.' So I resolved to be diligent and loyal in my prayer life, in self-denial, and in everything that was demanded of me."* [4] Fr Hillewaere wrote of her development at this time: *"Grace does not lose its grip on her but assists her in the difficult battle against the dangers and temptations of the world."* [5]

In these years Julia had to live in a secular environment. She saw the

---

[1] Cf. D. DE KEYZER, *"Madame est servie"*, p. 353.
[2] Cf. *ibid.*, pp. 297-298, and L. ALAERTS, *Door eigen werk sterk*. Geschiedenis van de kajotters en kajotsters in Vlaanderen 1924-1967, Leuven: Kadoc - Kajottershuis 2004, 417f. and pp. 464-466.
[3] Cf. L. Vos et al., *De christeljike arbeidersjeugd*, p. 415.
[4] Extracts from Mother Julia's account, 1935.
[5] *Ibid.*

material wealth of some families. She experienced the possibilities offered
to people by the increasing levels of prosperity, but also the dangers to
faith and Christian life that were bound up with such a situation. She was
not spared from participation in the struggle between serving the spirit of
God and the spirit of the world.

Things did not go well for her, when she worked for one childless
couple. She felt lonely and never got enough to eat: *"Apart from being
spoken to once a day to be given my instructions, I was completely ignored.
My health began to suffer, because I had to work so hard. Sometimes I was
extremely hungry. I realised that it was incumbent on me to leave that place."* [6]
In an attempt to persuade her to reconsider her decision to resign, her
employers offered to double her wages. However, she did not accept this
tempting offer, but simply asked the question: *"Wasn't I worth just as much
then as now?"* [7]

But Julia also had positive and rewarding experiences. Although still
young, she was given great responsibility in one family with seven children
in the French town of Tourcoing. The youngest child had just been born
and the mother was ill in bed. The grandparents also lived with the family.
The day was long. Julia worked from early in the morning until late in
the evening, caring for everyone in the house. Because of the way she
handled herself and worked around the house, she was able to foster a
happy atmosphere in the family, caring for the children, and including
all the family members in the various household tasks in a mutually
supportive way. She felt that she was completely accepted by this family:
*"We were a family, truly a family: in caring for each other, helping each other,
and working out together what was best both for us all and for each of us
individually."* [8]

Whilst Julia was with this family she became better acquainted with
the French language. She asked the children entrusted to her to care to
correct her mistakes, and they were more than happy to take on the role
of teacher. She rejoiced over any improvement and let the children know
how thankful she was. In this way, the relationship between Julia and the
children deepened. They loved her and would spontaneously help her,
where they could. Julia had become like a mother to the children. She had
a great influence on their upbringing, because she knew how to balance

[6] *Ibid.*
[7] Recollections of Mother Julia, written down 26 April 2002.
[8] Conversation with Mother Julia, 30 November 1993.

gentleness and firmness. Even in old age she remembered this family very well: *"At that time I learnt amongst other things what it means to be a mother. When I talk about it now, I feel fifty years younger. The grandparents became younger by the day. They had a lot to do, and felt useful. None of the children, or anyone else, ever went through a crisis. They didn't have time for that, and neither did I. Where there is love, service is easy. I was only just sixteen years old at this time."* [9]

In her years in domestic service, Julia would occasionally spend a few days at home with her parents. Her ever-watchful mother noticed that a young man was interested in her. As soon as Julia came home, he would come to visit. He also sought opportunities to meet her outside. According to Julia: *"Sometimes he came up to me in the street and spoke to me. But since I was not thinking of an intimate friendship, I was not concerned about this. Perhaps he spoke to me, because we were somewhat alike. That was my only thought and gave me self-confidence."* [10] Her mother heard about these meetings, and took her daughter to task: *"I was told off at home, but kept silent, and was considered all the more guilty. They thought that I did not want to tell the truth."* [11]

Given this situation, Julia was pleased when she was asked to accompany a sick mother's two children to the North Sea coast. During this stay in Het Zoute-aan-Zee, near the town of Knokke, God once again sent her the gift of a profound peace. He let her experience His glory in the beauty and stillness of nature and find tranquillity in a small chapel in the midst of the sand dunes.

The chapel of Het Zoute aan Zee at Knokke

Fr Hillewaere reported: *"She remained by the sea for five months in a small and remote resort. It was to be a time of contemplation and reflection."* [12] And Julia wrote: *"The stillness that permeated the place did me good. I craved it. Never before had I found nature so beautiful, so idyllic. How the broad sweep of forests and dunes spoke to me. In their midst dwelt the 'Solitary One',*

[9] *Ibid.*
[10] Extracts from Mother Julia's account, 1935.
[11] *Ibid.*
[12] *Ibid.*

View of the North Sea

Dune at the beach

often left alone in the Tabernacle! It was so still in the little chapel, which was rarely visited by anybody. I felt myself drawn to it. Everything here seemed to speak to me with such love and intimacy, even the vast and wonderful expanse of the sea. Everything bore witness to God's greatness, wisdom, omnipotence, goodness and beauty. I listened and learnt to love nature, from which I had received so much and which called me to contemplation. In the silence my soul had clearly heard the voice of grace. From now on I would follow the way of silent listening, in which I would discover God and get to know myself." [13]

During this period Julia continually took refuge with the Mother of the Lord. From her childhood she had been deeply devoted to Mary. And as she grew up she experienced more and more her motherly presence. She wrote to Fr Hillewaere: *"Do you know how I learn and am able to respond to everything, how I discovered the mystery of love? Through Mary, my mother. What bliss it is to be her child! Her love is so great and so creative. She is always ready with her counsel and answers, perhaps not always immediately, but in that case I simply wait for her response."* [14]

At Christmas 1928, Julia had to undergo an operation unexpectedly. She was obliged to give up her position, and was admitted to hospital in Menin. She experienced once more God's call to a life of greater dedication: *"It was just a few days before the lovely Christmas festivities. The infant Jesus did not want to invite me to contemplate the mystery of love in the crib, but wanted rather to allow me to experience something quite different: the mystery of love on the cross. Directly above my bed hung a large cross. It seemed to me that the suffering Jesus was always looking at me, whenever I glanced up at him. Our gazes met and each was aware of what the other was thinking. I felt*

---

[13] *Ibid.*
[14] *Ibid.*

that my love was not supernatural. I loved created things too much. I made the earnest resolution to change more profoundly and to begin a new life. I decided to end each day with an examination of conscience. From now on the hill of Calvary would teach me the love of sacrifice. The yearning to enter a convent became very strong again." [15]

In the midst of her many trials and tribulations, Julia knew that she was being protected and led by the Lord: *"My childhood and youth were marked by bodily and spiritual privation. But, at the same time, I encountered God's merciful justice, His sovereign guidance and saving love, His kingly omnipotence, with which He leads everything to its goal: to the glorification of the Father in the rebuilding of his kingdom on earth."* [16]

[15] *Ibid.*
[16] Mother Julia's notes, 1985.

VI. God's intervention in the cinema

It was the year 1929. Julia was in service with the industrialist, Adriaen De Clerck, and his wife, in Kortrijk, not far from Geluwe: *"I was alone, preparing the house for the newly weds. On her arrival the young bride handed me responsibility for the running of the household. Thus, I had complete freedom as to how I went about my duties."* [1] Julia quickly gained the respect of the couple. Because she performed her work so well, she was given the opportunity to attend Mass frequently. She thought seriously at this time about God's plan for her life.

One day, out of gratitude, Mme De Clerck gave her a cinema ticket, suggesting that she go to see the film, 'King of Kings', which portrayed the life of Jesus. Julia accepted the offer out of friendship, even though she did not consider it appropriate to go to the cinema during Lent. This film had been made in the USA in 1927 and was considered a masterpiece. The Lord was to use it to enter powerfully once more into her life.

Julia wrote about this event: *"It was during Lent in 1929. The film, 'King of Kings' was showing. It was a good film. I was in a cinema, but had gone reluctantly.*

Images from the film 'King of Kings' (1927): Mary Magdalene at the feet of Jesus

The Last Supper

---
[1] Extracts from Mother Julia's account, 1935.

I was doing it just to please Mme De Clerck. It was then that I received the grace of my conversion. How profoundly my soul was touched. I will never forget it: Jesus' look and His words as he took leave of His mother, His words to Mary Magdalene, to Peter, the triumphant entry into Jerusalem, the Last Supper, His testament, His apostles, and then the drama of His suffering! I left before the end of the film. Above me the sky was beautiful, full of stars, and around me a pleasant evening stillness. Everything appeared to be in harmony and drew me irresistibly to Him, and yet I felt ashamed of myself. I understood and felt that the Lord was calling me to something – clearly and without any reservation. A penetrating light had overwhelmed me. God's merciful love had taken possession of my soul and of my whole being with an attraction that was both strong and gentle. At that moment I gave myself totally to God, just as I was. In so far as my conscience could grasp that evening what it involved, I committed myself to fighting the good fight, to a life of more profound self-renunciation and denial." [2]

This spiritual enlightenment marked a decisive turning point in the life of Julia, who was then eighteen years old. She always considered this intervention of God as the call of grace to a more profound conversion and a more complete commitment. Immediately on her return from the cinema she made drastic changes to her way of life. For many years she had aimed to live a life based on faith. But with this new experience she was struck profoundly by God's holiness and by the magnitude of His merciful and just love.

Jesus crowned with thorns

In Jesus Christ, the King of Kings, she could see her life anew – with its good and less good sides. She recognised more clearly the imperfections that stood in the way of an exclusive love of the Lord: *"On the same evening I tidied up my room. I put away all those things that seemed unnecessary, so that I would no longer be attached to them. I noticed for the first time how fond I was of so many small and unimportant things. I took the cross down from the wall and wrote on the back of it, 'For You, O Jesus, help me!'*

[2] Letters of Mother Julia, 8 February 1949 and 27 April 1979. Extracts from Mother Julia's account, 1935.

I made the decision to get up everyday at 5.30 am. I resolved to go to holy Mass daily and to meditate on an episode from the life and suffering of Jesus for half an hour before the Mass. From the next day I set out still more resolutely on the way of internal and external self-denial and practised living in the presence of God. I found great help and strength in holy communion." [3]

God chose the medium of film, so important in people's lives in the twentieth century, in order to awaken in Julia a longing for holiness. The loving gaze of Jesus had touched her soul.
She said a radical 'Yes' to the Lord and set out on the arduous, but delightful, way of daily conversion, supported by God's power and love. She fought the good fight with determination and patience. She knew: *"Conversion is not the work of one day, nor is it our own work."* [4] Julia entered into a wide-ranging confrontation with those aspects of her character, which still required purification and transformation.

Christ on the way of the cross

She had learnt from St Paul to place her complete trust in God's merciful love in all her spiritual trials. She realised more than before that the struggle for personal sanctity must be permeated by, and surrounded in, this trust: *"Sometimes I would feel an urge to devote myself to the Lord even more, to surrender myself without reserve to His unappreciated love, but this thought frightened me and I hesitated."* However, the Lord sent her strength and courage: *"I recognised that I was being presented with the free choice between two ways, with both of which I was acquainted. If you love me, take up your cross and follow me (see Mt 10:28). I rose up and chose the way that leads to the house of the Father. I asked to love like Mary Magdalene and to be repentant like Peter. There will be joy at the return of a sinner, for in him will shine God's merciful love, which was revealed to us in His work of redemption. It seemed to me that I was now being carried forward by this love."* [5]

---

[3] Letter of Mother Julia, 8 February 1949.
[4] Extracts from Mother Julia's account, 1935.
[5] *Ibid.*

VII. The fall down the stairs

In Kortrijk Julia set about her household tasks with joy, and tried to give her wholehearted support to the young Mme De Clerck, who was expecting her first child.

One day, when Julia was cleaning the staircase that led to the first floor, someone rang the front doorbell. Julia ran downstairs to open the door. As she did so, she slipped, tumbled down several of the steps and fell on to an iron bucket at the bottom of the stairs. She felt an intense pain: *"Suddenly, like a flash of lightning, my body was struck by suffering through what to human eyes would appear to be an insignificant event. But in this instant Jesus was standing by me. Yes, it was like that. I saw what was coming and heard the Master's voice deep within me, calling me to climb the Mount of Calvary with Him."* [1]

The birth of Mme De Clerck's baby was imminent. As was her way, Julia wished to avoid anything that would upset her employer. So she did not complain about the consequences of her accident. In fact, she herself was not aware of the seriousness of her condition. When the pain became more bearable after a few days, she hoped that she was getting better.

With a fall down these stairs started a time of suffering for Julia

Shortly afterwards, Julia's mother became so ill that it was thought her life was in danger. Julia was suddenly called back home, and looked after her mother with great love. In spite of her own suffering, she wanted to keep vigil by the sick bed alone. Eventually, there was some improvement in her mother's health.

Julia's pain reared up again, and after several medical tests it was

---

[1] Extracts from Mother Julia's account, 1935.

Julia some months after the accident

Mrs Madeleine Tiberghien-d'Halluin with her daughter Denise and her granddaughter Françoise

discovered that she had broken and splintered some of her ribs. This led to recurrent bouts of inflammation. Some time later she was given permission by her doctor to return to Kortrijk, in order to assist Mme De Clerck in the weeks after the birth. However, it was not long before Julia had to return home once more on account of the effects of her fall. In the coming years Julia was to experience great bodily and spiritual afflictions. Her health was a continual state of flux. After hopeful indications of recovery would inevitably come new setbacks.

In October 1929, Julia took over the position of her newly married sister, Augusta, who worked for the distinguished Tiberghien family in Tourcoing, a town in France. Mrs Tiberghien had lost her husband, the respected manager of a textile mill. The young widow had a good reputation and was well known for her commitment to the faith. She became very fond of Julia and was worried about her poor health, helping her obtain further medical examinations and treatments. But as she showed no real signs of improvement, Julia had to give up this position as well and return home, much to Mrs Tiberghien's regret. Julia wrote: *"Mrs Tiberghien wanted to be a mother to me and tried to discourage me from leaving."* [2]

In January 1930, Julia joined the 'Apostolate of the Sick', an association made up of a large number of sick people. Together with them she sought to offer her suffering for the salvation of souls:[3] *"Quite by chance I was given a letter to read from the 'Apostolate of the Sick'. I was impressed. I did not just want to offer up my*

[2] *Ibid.*

[3] Cf. INTERDIOCESAAN CENTRUM (Ed.), *Katholiek Jaarboek voor België*, Brussels, privately printed 1958, p. 376.

suffering, but to be an apostle as well. I felt that Jesus was calling me to this. I was ready to be an apostle of Jesus in my illness. I was inexpressibly happy in this apostolate." [4]

In the same year, she underwent two operations in the hospital in Menin, but without obtaining the hoped for results. On account of her illness Julia was unable to take up paid employment for several years, but had to remain for most of the time in her parents' house. During this period one doctor informed her that she could not expect to live a long life. She became aware that the Lord was demanding from her the sacrifice of her health. She consented to this demand willingly: *"Since Jesus' love invited me, I gave myself to Him anew, offered up my health to him, and accepted everything that the future was to bring."* [5] The fall down the stairs had marked the decisive entrance of illness into Julia's life. Her body would never fully recover.

In 1930 Julia became a member of the 'Apostolate of the Sick'

On account of her attachment to God Julia had a powerful attraction for, and a lasting influence on, those who met her. Again and again, people seeking help turned to her, although it was not the normal practice at that time to seek spiritual guidance from a young woman. She gave the following advice to one person who knew her well and asked for help: *"If you have an argument with someone and feel hurt inside, it is good not to blame the other person too quickly. For it might be the case that the guilt, or a share of the guilt, lies with you. Perhaps the other person is knocking against your sharp corners. Oversensitivity often has its roots in wounded egotism."* [6] In the midst of her trials Julia remained sensitive to the spiritual needs of other people. Faith gave her the certainty that all that was happening to her was ultimately serving God's mysterious plan for her: *"I had found a hidden treasure in humiliation and suffering. In them I saw the path I had to follow."* [7]

---

[4] Extracts from Mother Julia's account, 1935.
[5] *Ibid.*
[6] Recollections of Mother Julia, written down 27 February 1990.
[7] Extracts from Mother Julia's account, 1935.

In spite of everything, Julia was not idle. In so far as her health permitted, she assisted her parents at home and worked as a seamstress for a company making serviettes and other items. She excelled in this work because of her proficiency and hard work. Whatever she produced was highly prized and regarded, so her employer testified, as of the best and finest quality. Julia was happy that she was able to support her family in this way.

These years were marked by great hardship. The crisis of the world economy in 1929 led to widespread poverty. Belgium was not spared. Unemployment increased dramatically. Even if people were fortunate enough to find employment, the pay was so low that they could barely afford the minimum necessary to sustain themselves.[8] Julia wrote: *"I tried to lighten the load of the burden I had placed on my parents, as far as I could, by taking in work at home. I didn't feel unemployed. From morning till evening, I busied myself with making whatever I could with my hands. In this way, I also had the opportunity to reflect on my life and to glimpse into the past and into the future."*[9]

The medical treatment of the ribs damaged by Julia's fall down the stairs had had little success. The injuries were healing very slowly, and occasionally the wounds would open up again. Julia was often consigned to her bed: *"But it was a time of great grace. During the many months of suffering I drew strength from sacrifice. In God's light I could see His merciful love and above all His goodness."*[10]

Julia felt herself drawn ever more to the contemplative life. At times she even considered joining one of the contemplative orders. But this was not possible, particularly on account of her health problems. So, on the 11 February 1934, she joined the Carmelite Third Order in Wervik. She loved the great Carmelite saints, especially Thérèse of the Child Jesus and Elizabeth of the Trinity, although she knew little of their lives. At that time it was usual for members of the Third Order to be given their own patron. Julia was entrusted to Elizabeth of the Trinity, who, like her, had been filled with a great love of the Apostle Paul. This Carmelite, who had died in 1906, became an important spiritual companion for Julia: *"She called me inwards. I mean, she led me deeper into the contemplative life. She helped me to step outside of the turbulent and restless world that*

---

[8] Cf. D. DE KEYZER, *"Madame est servie"*, p. 362.
[9] Extracts from Mother Julia's account, 1935.
[10] *Ibid.*

surrounded me. She taught me to listen to the merciful Heart of Jesus with longing and yearning." [11]

Looking back on the spiritual journey she had followed in childhood and adolescence, she wrote: *"Even in those years I received particular demonstrations of grace from the Lord. I was not conscious of this at the time. I didn't have, if I can put it like this, the slightest idea about the spiritual life, and I was unworthy of such demonstrations of grace. Perhaps I am not expressing myself very well: I was simply trying to love the Lord in my own way. I was not able to do it any other way, and we understood each other."* [12]

---

[11] Mother Julia's Notes, 17 May 1986.
[12] Letter of Mother Julia, 10 July 1948.

SECOND PART

Birth of a New Charism
(1934-1943)

VIII. The "Holy Covenant"

Whilst Julia followed events in Church and society, bringing them to the Lord in prayer in the stillness and simplicity of the little house in Geluwe, dark clouds massed over the landscape of international affairs. The prolonged economic crisis led to far reaching political changes in many countries. Dictators came to power with the promise of reducing unemployment and easing the hardship being experienced by many in society. On 30 January 1933, Adolf Hitler was appointed Chancellor of Germany. Soon afterwards came the implementation of the 'Gleichschaltung', the alignment of state, economy, culture and the whole of public life in the service of the goals of National Socialism.[1] In 1934 the watchwords of foreign policy were disarmament and security. In reality, re-armament was taking place everywhere. A series of international moves aimed at disarmament failed. The arms race was in full stride.

As a result of these developments there arose the so-called politics of alliance. The great powers tried to consolidate and increase their power through pacts and treaties. In one historical chronicle, it states: *"1934 was, therefore, a year of alliances between states: the German-Polish non-aggression pact, the Balkan pact between Greece, Yugoslavia, Rumania and Turkey, the Roman protocol between Italy, Austria and Hungary, the Baltic pact between Estonia, Latvia and Lithuania, and other treaties, designed to safeguard areas of influence and national security interests. With the great number of alliances conflicts of interest and tensions between the power blocks intensified. The danger of war increased."*[2]

For Julia, too, 1934 was a particularly significant year. Once more she was confined to her sick bed in her parent's house. On the Solemnity of the Sacred Heart she experienced *"a grace-filled light"*,[3] in which she encountered the Lord, crowned with thorns. Shaken to the depths of her

---

[1] Cf. E.C. Schütt, *Chronik 1933. Tag für Tag in Wort und Bild,* Die Chronik-Bibliothek des 20. Jahrhunderts, Vol. 33, ed. B. Harenberg, Dortmund: Chronik Verlag ²1993, p. 7.
[2] B. Polmann, *Chronik 1934. Tag für Tag in Wort und Bild,* Die Chronik-Bibliothek des 20. Jahrhunderts, Vol. 34, ed. B. Harenberg, Dortmund: Chronik Verlag ³1993, p. 7; cf. A. Palmer and H. Thomas, *Die Moderne Welt im Aufbruch,* pp. 213-218.
[3] Letter of Mother Julia, 8 February 1993.

soul by the suffering of Jesus on the cross and seized by the infinite love of His Heart, she was filled with inexpressible sorrow, and felt that Jesus wanted to bind her more closely to His Heart and was calling her to a life of commitment as His bride. Julia heard and accepted the invitation to share His loving thirst for souls, especially for souls willing to participate in the consecrated life. It seemed to her as if the divine love had taken possession of her heart. Filled with this love, she gave herself to the Lord for the good of the Church: *"The 'Yes' that I spoke to the Lord at that time, was like a 'Holy Covenant' with the incarnate Heart of Jesus, which perpetually offers Itself up in His body, the Church."* [4]

This experience of grace led Julia deeper into the work of redemption. Attracted by the love of the crucified Christ, she received greater insight into the mystery of the New Covenant that God had made with man. A few years earlier Saint Paul had led her to the Heart of Jesus and to His body, the Church. Now she grasped more profoundly in the love of the Heart of Jesus the meaning of the new and eternal Covenant, whose outstanding witness was Saint Paul. In this Covenant the sins of men are taken away (see Rom 11:27) and their hearts transformed and filled with the Holy Spirit (see Rom 5:5). The New Covenant is not a covenant of the letter, but a covenant of the Spirit (see 2 Cor 3:6), in which the children of God are led to true freedom (Gal 4:24).

It was through this 'Holy Covenant' that Julia attained a deeper union of love with the Lord. Later, when she was permitted to see the importance of this 'covenant', she wrote in a prayer:

> *"Jesus, my Lord and my Christ,*
> *You wanted to open to me the door of your heart,*
> *which is wounded by suffering*
> *and by the misdeeds of sinners.*
> *You have revealed to me the glorious mystery of the 'Covenant'*
> *that flows from Your merciful Heart.*
>
> *O Saviour, what trust,*
> *what grace, what abundant forgiveness!*
> *You always have pity on Your chosen people.*
> *Ceaselessly, You hear their cries and laments,*
> *And save them for eternal life.*

---

[4] Letter of Mother Julia, 6 June 1975.

To You be the honour and the glory
Both now and forever more.

You have bound me to You
In the grace of the 'Holy Covenant'.
May I live this great gift with You
in profound love.

Jesus, my King and my Bridegroom,
My life, my joy, my all,
Your Heart, burning with love,
is my resting place forever.
There You show me clearly the way
to follow You without fear or doubt.

Cloaked in Your mercifulness,
I give myself to Your law
And to Your commandments.
You have drawn me into a profound union with You
In order to share in the work of salvation
And to atone for the sins of the world." [5]

Julia experienced the 'Holy Covenant' as a completely unexpected gift from God, which filled her with thankfulness, reverence and awe. It helped to deepen and further develop the grace of baptism in her. The 'Holy Covenant' made her more conscious of the fact that she was living her life within the great history of salvation; a history illuminated again and again by the constant faithfulness of God in the face of man's unfaithfulness. In later years, she wrote: *"The 'Holy Covenant' should make us appreciate anew the history of salvation!"* [6] She was allowed to understand that the history of salvation extends to all times, and that God works great things in the hearts of those who follow His Son in faith, hope and love.

When Julia was given the 'Holy Covenant', she was still a young woman, not yet 24 years old. Even then, it was clear to her that the crown of thorns would continue to mark her life. United with Christ, Who atoned for the pride of the world with His crown of thorns, she heard in her conscience the invitation to make reparation voluntarily for the spiritual pride of men and to pray and suffer vicariously for many: *"I was allowed to understand*

---

[5] Enclosed with letter of Mother Julia, 19 April 1985.
[6] Mother Julia's Notes, 8 December 1985.

that the crown of thorns would be of great importance in my life. I accepted it. The significance of what it involved was made clear to me only later. I offered myself up as a sacrificial gift." [7]

At the same time the Lord awoke in her a thirst for souls. She bore witness to this with the following words: *"I was filled as it were with an unquenchable thirst to love Jesus and to make others love Him, by surrendering myself to a very profound purification and conversion in response to the mission he had gradually helped me to recognise and which developed in the grace and charism of The Work."* [8]

This loving thirst for souls was like a blazing fire in her heart. The willingness to share with priests the sacrifice of self for the salvation of souls permeated her whole being. She wrote to Fr Hillewaere: *"It is the most intimate desire of Jesus that there should develop and be formed still more*

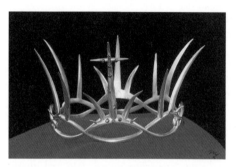

The glorified crown of thorns, emblem of The Spiritual Family The Work

souls, ready to sacrifice themselves completely for priests and at the side of priests." [9] In the spirit of Saint Paul she felt herself compelled to offer her life for the redemption of many *"as a living and holy sacrifice, pleasing to God"* (Rom 12:1).

This sacrifice was nothing other than her unconditional and loving commitment to Christ as his bride: *"When I gave my 'Yes' to the Lord in 1934, to serve His plan from then on, I entered at the same time into a new world, which was the Lord Himself, the crucified Son of Man, crowned with thorns, the King of this time and of all eternity, if I can put it like that. From then on I belonged to Him in a very special way. I became 'His'."* [10]

Towards the end of her life Julia bore testimony to the grace that she had received in 1934: *"My 'Yes' was like a milestone on the way to The Work. This charism was to develop in the midst of the signs of the times to stand with the Church, which found itself in a situation of adversity. This was how I saw and experienced it."* [11]

---

[7] Letter of Mother Julia, 6 June 1975.
[8] Letter of Mother Julia, 19 June 1984.
[9] Letter of Mother Julia, 1934.
[10] Letter of Mother Julia, 25 January 1992.
[11] Letter of Mother Julia, 8 February 1993.

IX. Further graces and trials

Julia spent most of the period from 1934 to 1938 in Geluwe on account of her illness. From time to time she was able to undertake some light tasks, helping around her parents' house and taking in work to provide some financial assistance to her family. The grace of the Covenant that she had received on the feast of the Sacred Heart in 1934 was initially a purely personal gift. As yet, Julia was unaware of her future mission to be the means by which a new community would arise in the Church.

At this time she increasingly felt a desire to live a contemplative life of prayer and silence. But it was clear to her that her ill health might make her a burden to a religious community. One day she was told that a Carmelite convent was willing to accept her in spite of her poor health. After a period of prayer, reflection and calm consideration she realized that her condition would require her to be exempted from parts of the Carmelite rule and that the consequences for a religious community would be considerable. For this reason she said of the possibility of her entry into the Carmel: *"I knew that I did not have the necessary good health and that the sacrifices involved would place too great a burden on the Carmel."* [1] Thus she freely renounced the opportunity to enter the Carmel and offered her longing for the contemplative life to the Lord as a sacrifice: *"He did not spare me these purifying and sanctifying trials, but led me to a most profound renunciation. God had demanded from me the sacrifice of my future, the sacrifice of my vocation."* [2]

Her neighbours were sympathetic towards her suffering. Julia reported: *"The neighbours made a novena for me twice, when I was very ill. For nine days they made a pilgrimage on foot to Dadizele. They set off in the morning at four or five o'clock, in order to be able to participate in the first holy Mass of the day at 5.30 or 6 o'clock. This was the commendable custom, when someone in the neighbourhood was very ill. People still believed in the power of prayer and sacrifice."* [3]

---

[1] Conversation with Mother Julia, 5 August 1989.
[2] Letter of Mother Julia, 27 April 1979.
[3] Mother Julia's Notes, 1985.

Julia wanted just one thing: to be a compliant instrument in the hands of God, to give herself over completely to His guidance, and to serve His plan. She wanted to follow the King, crowned with thorns, unconditionally, even when she could not see how her longing for the consecrated life in the grace of the 'Holy Covenant' would take concrete shape. Every day she sought to bear witness to her love for the Lord and her neighbour: *"I strive for perfection in everything. I want to avoid anything that could displease Jesus. I long only to love Jesus sincerely and completely and to strive to make others love Him. I am convinced that Jesus knows the hearts of men through and through and does not withhold his grace from us, if we are ready for anything and co-operate with grace. His love for us is infinite, especially when we seek to respond to it honestly. Is it not simple to do every day what he demands, to fulfil one's duty to God and one's neighbour faithfully and promptly? Good and beautiful thoughts, feelings and resolutions alone will not bring me peace."* [4]

Again and again, at this time of searching and struggling to discern her concrete place in the Church, Julia found comfort in Mary, the Mother of the Lord: *"I have always had a great love for her and have often experienced her help. I no longer do anything without her. She teaches me and moulds me according to the will of Jesus, and that is quite plain. With Mary I learn to love the will of Jesus, to receive everything, to accept everything and to give everything back. In this way, every day, every hour, every moment becomes a Magnificat, a Fiat. In order to understand Mary, we must be her children, humble in spirit and free from self, content with everything, including ourselves, just as we are. When our love is genuine, pure, sincere, and willing to serve, without selfishness and self-centred desires, then we will live in Jesus with Mary, our Mother."* [5]

Further difficulties did not pass Julia by. Her mother's health worsened significantly. On Palm Sunday, 1935, she received the Sacrament of the Sick, as it was thought that her death was imminent. After a brief period of remission, she died on 16 December of the same year. On her memorial card it reads: *"Her faith was strong and lively. In the midst of many trials her trust in divine Providence did not waver."* [6] Unexpectedly, on 14 February 1937, Julia's father also passed away. It was said of him: *"He was a man who feared God. The faith was rooted in his soul like an oak in the rocks."* [7] Her

---

[4] Extracts from Mother Julia's account, 1935.
[5] *Ibid.*
[6] Mrs Valentine Verhaeghe-Rosé's memorial card.
[7] Mr Henri Verhaeghe's memorial card.

hope in eternal life helped Julia to accept the painful departure of her parents. She had always possessed a great respect for them: *"As a child, I never heard my parents quarrel. As I got older, I recognised more clearly their individual peculiarities, but unity and love bound them together."* [8] Julia was always thankful to her parents for giving her so much.

From where did she obtain the strength to keep faithfully to her solitary path? The fire of love burnt in her heart. She wrote: *"The Lord says, 'Without me you can do nothing.' He never leaves us alone, even when it appears that He has separated Himself from us. How true this is! How I want to praise Him and thank Him, for leading me through the mill of suffering and alienation! It was there that he sent me His merciful light. God is a father. He is love. In His love He sent me Saint Paul as a support and a guide."* [9]

Julia's parents a few years before they died

Through the Apostle Paul, Julia became acquainted with the mystery of the Church. It was at this time that God sent her special graces, which led to the further development of the 'Holy Covenant'. While her mother received the Sacrament of the Sick on Palm Sunday, 1935, God allowed her to grasp more deeply the riches that lie hidden in the maternal heart of the Church: *"I underwent an inner experience, which revealed to me the mystery of the Church, the Mystical Body of Christ, our holy Mother, as well as the inexpressible treasure of the Sacraments that we have been given in God's merciful love, particularly in the priesthood, the Eucharist, in the Sacrament of Penance and in the Sacrament of the Sick. It was as if this inner experience had ignited a fire in me that burns and illumines: a strong love for this Mother, the Church, who is immaculate and powerful."* [10]

Julia was seized once more by the supernatural greatness and beauty of the Church. Since her encounter with Paul she had borne in her heart a love for the Church. This love matured with the years and became ever more pure, strong and complete.

While the mystery of the Church began to take hold of Julia's soul,

---

[8] Conversation with Mother Julia, 8 February 1996.
[9] Letter of Mother Julia, 27 April 1979.
[10] *Ibid.*

the flourishing Catholic Action movement was influencing the life of the people of God in many countries. Catholic Action had its origins in a wide-ranging Catholic movement in Europe, which had cast its spell over many priests and lay people, encouraging renewal in the life of the Church. The influential French priest, Félicité Lamennais (1782-1854), was the first to use the term, 'Catholic Action'. However, parts of this movement, including Lamennais himself,[11] were influenced by liberal ideas and came to oppose the official teaching of the Church.

Later, in different circumstances, Popes Leo XIII and Pius X revived the idea of 'Catholic Action'. But it was with Pope Pius XI from 1925 onwards that Catholic Action developed into a concrete organisation, assuming its mature form.[12] This pope knew from the beginning of his

Pope Pius XI

pontificate that Catholic Action could be a powerful force for renewal. So, in his Encyclical, *Ubi Arcano* (1922), he laid the foundation for the amalgamation of many initiatives and movements within the lay apostolate under the leadership of the Church's hierarchy. Catholic Action was to act as a defence against the new tendencies that arose after the First World War, which desired to construct a society without God and to banish religion from public life. Among the fundamental principles underlying Catholic Action, the pope spoke of subordination to the all-encompassing lordship of Christ, conformity to the universality of the Church as a means to overcoming nationalism and religious liberalism, a deeper understanding of the Church as the mystical body of Christ, and a new co-operation between clergy and laity and between the various Catholic associations and movements.

Catholic Action spread through many countries. It brought about a revitalisation of religious life, a new enthusiasm for the Church, as well as a deeper understanding of the necessity of apostolic involvement in

---

[11] Cf. R. AUBERT, 'Das Erwachen der katholischen Lebenskraft' in H. JEDIN (Ed.), *Handbuch der Kirchengeschichte*, Band VI/1: *Die Kirche zwischen Revolution und Restauration*, Freiburg-Basel-Wien: Herder 1971, 279-282; R. AUBERT, 'Die erste Phase des katholischen Liberalismus' in *ibid.*, pp. 320-347; ALAERTS, *Door eigen werk sterk*, p. 29.
[12] Cf. J. VERSCHEURE, 'Katholische Aktion' in J. HÖFER and K. RAHNER (Eds.), *Lexikon für Theologie und Kirche*, Vol. 6, Freiburg: Herder ²1961, 902ff.

society. The influence of Catholic Action did not just affect the inner life of the Church. On the contrary, the Christian faith suddenly gained a significance in public life that it had not possessed for a long time. Thus, there arose the opportunity to win back to Christianity sections of society, for instance the working classes, that had been lost to the Church in the previous decades. It was fundamentally a question of helping people, through a new evangelisation, not to give in to the newly emerging paganism.

Fr Hillewaere worked as a chaplain to several groups within Catholic Action. Julia saw in this movement a gift of the Holy Spirit, and, as Pope Pius XI had desired, God's answer to the difficulties in Church and society, and a new possibility for the laity to co-operate in the apostolic mission of the Church, infusing the world with the spirit of the Gospel. She wrote of the significance of Catholic Action: *"It came at God's appointed hour as a summons and a gift of His never failing love and of His merciful kindness towards men. It appeared to me to be a sign of God's powerful intervention."* [13]

---

[13] Letter of Mother Julia, 6 June 1975.

X. Joseph Cardijn and the Young Catholic Workers

In Belgium, in the years after the First World War, the movement, known as the Young Catholic Workers, grew up under the influence and direction of Joseph (later Cardinal) Cardijn (1882-1967). Cardijn set out to apply the principles of Catholic Action to the life and experience of young workers. With a core group of young people he wanted to respond to the great challenge of the time by winning over the masses. In 1920, Belgium had approximately seven million inhabitants, of whom one million were young people between fourteen and twenty-one years of age. The First World War had particularly affected young workers, who experienced great spiritual, moral and social hardship with little hope of a better future.[1]

Cardijn and his colleagues wanted to lead young people back to the ideal of the Christian life, to make them aware of their dignity as children of God and to search for solutions to their social problems. The first generation of this movement contained not only young workers, but also priests and members of the middle classes, who were particularly concerned with the religious and personal formation of young people in the working environment. In 1924 the male, and in 1925 the female, sections of the Young Catholic Worker movement were established at a national level.[2] However, Cardijn's pioneering initiatives were not understood by everyone at the time, and, as a result of the increasing ecclesiastical and social tensions, Cardijn sought an audience with Pope Pius XI. At this meeting the Pope expressed his full support for Cardijn.[3] From a religious perspective, the Young Catholic Workers initially came under the influence of the Eucharistic Crusade of Fr Poppe. But, at the beginning of the 1930s, they moved away from this form of spirituality, since it was not sufficiently suited to Cardijn's apostolic objectives, although some of Fr Poppe's spiritual principles were retained.[4]

---

[1] Cf. E. Arnould, A. Boulvin, L. Bragard et al. (Eds.), *Va libérer mon peuple! (Ex 3,10). La pensée de Joseph Cardijn*, Paris-Bruxelles: Editions Ouvrières-Vie Ouvrière. 1982, pp. 15-17; L. Alaerts, *Door eigen werk sterk*, pp. 81 and 83ff.

[2] M. Fievez and J. Meert, *Cardijn*, Bruxelles: Vie Ouvrière ³1978, p. 81.

[3] Cf. *ibid.*, 74f., and L. Alaerts, *Door eigen werk sterk*, 61f. and pp. 65-67.

[4] Cf. L. Alaerts, *Door eigen werk sterk*, 240ff.

The Young Catholic Workers were very influential at this time of world economic crisis,[5] as they were in a position to provide hope and meaning to many young people in the midst of all the moral and social hardships. They became increasingly active and quickly spread throughout Belgium and other countries.[6]

Although she could clearly see the positive influence of the Young Catholic Workers, Julia was aware of the difficulties associated with this movement, and increasingly saw the spiritual dangers to which some of its leaders and members were exposed. As a result of their sudden growth and their eagerness to win over the masses,[7] there was a real lack of maturity and stability. Julia wrote: *"The apostolate lacks an inner life. Everything has to be tested and purified first in the continual good fight. Many are not sufficiently aware that they must engage with perseverance in the active apostolate, first by example and then by words and deeds. This is the case in particular for those who take on a special commitment."*[8]

Julia was also concerned about the formation of the movement's young leadership. At the beginning of the 1930s the apostolic goals of the movement changed and, as Leen Alaerts in an historical study affirmed, took on *"a propagandistic rather than educational value".*[9] The young people were called upon to analyse the various areas of life according to the principle, 'see – judge – act', and to gain many new members. This led to a change of emphasis in the movement, which became more *"a means of conquest and less a method of formation".*[10] Julia repeatedly referred to the fact that for the young there were not enough capable people in positions of responsibility with sufficient foresight to meet the challenge of guiding and forming their conscience: *"It's a matter of an ongoing and more fundamental formation, which goes beyond the movement itself. It's a matter of formation in a completely comprehensive sense, of a 'personal formation'."*[11] For Julia, it was always a matter of concern to prepare young people for their life's journey in following Christ more closely, whether in marriage or in any other state of life.

Fr Hillewaere was a personal friend and colleague of Joseph Cardijn. In his pastoral activity within Catholic Action, and particularly within

---

[5] Cf. *ibid.*, p. 157.
[6] Cf. *ibid.*, pp. 151ff., 157-163, 166-171, 173, and 219ff.
[7] Cf. *ibid.*, pp. 106, 122, 151-153, 156, and 159.
[8] Letter of Mother Julia, 25 August 1934.
[9] L. ALAERTS, *Door eigen werk sterk*, p. 159.
[10] *Ibid.*
[11] Letter of Mother Julia, 25 September 1943.

the Young Catholic Workers, he strove to foster whatever was of religious, social or educational value and to conserve the original spirit of the movement in line with the wishes of the Church's hierarchy. At the same time, some developments caused him concern, especially in relation to the leadership of the movement.[12] He felt obliged to speak frequently about his concerns with Canon Cardijn, who was to some extent of the same mind. Having visited several groups of the Young Catholic Workers, he later wrote: *"I am alarmed, because the formation of the young leadership has been neglected. Goodwill is there, as well as an admirable readiness, but there are shortcomings in their knowledge of the movement and of the application of principles, in their spiritual and moral life, in their lifestyle and in their discipline."*[13]

The future Cardinal Joseph Cardijn and Fr Arthur Cyriel Hillewaere in 1937

Moreover, one of Cardijn's friends, supported by others who also held the Young Catholic Worker movement in high regard, had already in 1932 detected another danger: *"It seems to me that in their great zeal, which I respect and admire, the attitude of the leadership of the Young Workers to their movement is 'totalitarian'. I think that this is gradually creating a spirit, which, if it continues to grow, will bring with it excesses and dangers. This totalitarian spirit leads to a failure to work together with other Catholic organisations and initiatives, which do not belong to Catholic Action, but are necessary for the common good. It also leads to a lack of interest in other causes and concerns*

---

[12] Cf. L. ALAERTS, *Door eigen werk sterk*, pp. 273ff.

[13] ARCHIVES GENERALES DU ROYAUME, "Fonds-Cardijn". To this part of the archive there are two inventories: M. FIEVEZ and F. WINDELS-ROSART, *Inventaris van het Fonds-Cardijn*, ed. Ministerie van onderwijs and Ministère de l'éducation nationale, Algemeen Rijksarchief and Rijksarchief in de Provincies, Algemeen Rijksarchief, translated by C. De Cuyper and K. Goris, Brussels: privately printed by Algemeen Rijksarchief, 1986; M. FIEVEZ, A. BRICTEUX and A. ERICZ, *Complément à l'inventaire Cardijn* (Archives générales du Royaume instruments de recherche à tirage limité 409), Brussels: privately printed by Archives générales du Royaume 1996, Dossier No 1825, listed in *Inventaris van het Fonds-Cardijn*, p. 124.

within the Church. Catholic Action does not comprise the entire activity of the Church, nor do the Young Catholic Workers provide the only way of reaching a higher goal. They must adapt and subordinate themselves. I believe that these failures of the movement will inflict great harm both within and without." [14]

Julia suffered as a result of such developments. Her inner sense of God's action in salvation history allowed her to understand how important it is to serve God's plan, to honour Him in the hidden events of everyday life, not to shy away from struggle and sacrifice in apostolic service, and at the same time to be able to live in expectation of 'the hour of God'. Fr Hillewaere sustained and provided direction for her conscience with great respect, particularly from 1935 onwards, as it became clearer to Julia that it was God's will that she should consult him about her interior life. She was thankful for his direction and followed it obediently, co-operating with the grace of the charism, which was growing silently in her heart.

Five years before her death, she wrote: *"It seems to me that this period was a time of deep conversion and purification, in which the Lord wanted to remodel my entire person and my entire being on Him through interior and exterior growth, in order to prepare me to comply with His plan and His decrees."* [15]

---

[14] *Ibid.*, Dossier No 1820/3, listed in *Inventaris van het Fonds-Cardijn*, p. 124.
[15] Letter of Mother Julia, 25 January 1992.

XI. The foundation of The Work

In 1938 the situation in Europe was very menacing. Adolf Hitler, who was following an increasingly aggressive political path, took over as supreme commander of the German armed forces.[1] His lust for power filled people with fear. Was a new World War about to break out?

Along with many others Fr Hillewaere was alarmed at these developments and sought to stand with the people in their time of need. He became increasingly concerned at the political situation in Europe and at the state of affairs within Catholic Action. In addition to his pastoral responsibilities in the parish, he had for many years worked with different groups in Catholic Action as spiritual director and confessor. He organised retreats, days of recollection and talks, putting all his effort into his work with young people. As a result of this involvement, he began to realise that the Young Catholic Workers had to some extent moved away from their original goals. He experienced more and more conflicts of conscience, and had to distance himself inwardly from certain developments, without giving up his willing involvement in the movement. He saw in particular the need for a number of well-prepared leaders, who would combine maturity and spirituality with apostolic engagement in the world.

He was very taken with the idea of consecrated women, who would form a nucleus in the young women's groups and take on leadership activities alongside priests.[2] At the same time, he was attracted by the grace that was quietly growing in one of the young people in his parish. Because he sought to follow his conscience sincerely and through his studies had developed an understanding of spiritual development, he recognised grace at work in the life of the young Julia Verhaeghe, and saw here an answer to the questions and difficult issues which were besetting him.[3]

---

[1] Cf., E.C. SCHÜTT, *Chronik 1938. Tag für Tag in Wort und Bild*. Die Chronik-Bibliothek des 20. Jahrhunderts, Vol. 38, ed. by B. Harenberg, Dortmund: Chronik-Verlag 1988, p. 7.
[2] Cf. Notes of Fr Hillewaere at the beginning of 1938.
[3] Extracts from Mother Julia's account, January 1938.

As he was celebrating Mass on 18 January 1938, in this chapel of the Sisters of Our Lady of Bunderen in Geluwe, Fr Hillewaere received the grace of the 'Holy Covenant'

He celebrated his fiftieth birthday on 18 January 1938. During holy Mass, he offered up his concerns about the developments within Catholic Action at the altar. Uniting himself with Christ's sacrifice of Himself for the sins of the world, he implored God to show him His will. At that moment, he experienced an inner call to offer up his life as a priest for the renewal of Catholic Action and for the development of the charism of The Work, the growth of which he had been involved in as a spiritual father for many years. Julia expressed this significant experience in Fr Hillewaere's life in the following words: *"It was then that the merciful God revealed to him the decrees of His will concerning His Work: the charism that He wished to give in response to the needs of the people of God."* [4] Fr Hillewaere's consent was a pure act of faith, a placing of himself in trust at God's disposal. In this act of commitment he partook of the grace of the 'Holy Covenant', which Julia had received four years previously through God's merciful love.

Until the end of his life, he remained conscious of the significance of this act of divine providence. Thus, many years later, he wrote in a letter: *"The 18 January 1938 was not just my birthday, but also the day on which I gave the Lord the rest of my life for The Work."* [5]

On the same morning of the 18 January Julia was filled with an inexpressible joy. She was able to unite herself spiritually with Fr Hillewaere's celebration of the sacrifice of the Mass, so that decades later she could still say with deep emotion: *"In that Mass, in accordance with God's plan, there truly arose in our souls a profound and intimate union. I don't know how else I can convey it or express it. It was so glorious and so wonderful, that it transcended all human thought and knowledge."* [6]

---

[4] Notes of Mother Julia, 18 January 1992.
[5] Letter of Fr Hillewaere, 19 January 1967.
[6] Mother Julia's Notes, 6 June 1976.

Dieu m'a donné comme un cœur nouveau. le fait m'a placée dans une toute autre situation face à la vie dans ce monde et face à mes relations avec Dieu. à partir de ce moment je voyais et je vois la vie, les choses autour de moi et en moi-même, tout autrement. —

Julia's manuscript of the text quoted here below

The love of God filled her whole being: *"God gave me a new heart, so to speak. This fact placed me in a completely different situation in relation to God and the world. From that moment on I saw life and the things around me and within me in a quite different light."* [7]

Both Julia and Fr Hillewaere recognised that, in this hour of grace, God had bound and cemented together the gift of personal charism and the grace of the priestly office in a mutually complementary way for the building up of the Church.

Julia was twenty-seven years old at the time. For many years, the Lord had been preparing her for this day, which she always called the birthday of The Work, and on which God again unexpectedly intervened in her life: *"It was an event that marked a great turning point in my life. My soul was allowed to see a mystery of love, like a bride, who sees and understands her bridegroom's hopes for the future. God's deepest mysteries lie at the origins of the vocation. In the beginning, there was nothing – except the grace of God with us. It was thus that the vocation saw the light of day."* [8]

It was clear to Julia that the founding of The Work was bound up with a new responsibility. God had entrusted her with a new charism for the Church. From now on, her life was given over exclusively

Mother Julia, some years after the foundation of The Work

[7] Letter of Mother Julia, 6 January 1980.
[8] Mother Julia's Notes, 6 June 1976 and 11 January 1970. Letter of Mother Julia, 20 January 1963.

to being the 'Mother' of The Work, sacrificing herself completely for its further development. She wrote: *"The 18 January is a day of grace and profound thankfulness for the light and the graces through which my whole being became The Work."* [9]

It had never occurred to Mother Julia that she would bring a community to birth. But God had determined that a new charism would enter the Church through her. She bore testimony to this in the following words: *"It pleased God to choose me according to His Will to be an instrument of His Work. I feel an urge from within to make it clear that I never had the idea or the intention of founding a 'Work' myself. In the situation and conditions in which I found myself, it was impossible for me to come up with such thoughts and ideas. But God had cured me of, and rescued me from, the spirit of the times, as He did others of my generation. He had lit in me a great love for the Church, the Mystical Body of Christ. I have founded nothing. When Jesus Christ founded the Church, everything was founded. He just needs people to live this foundation profoundly – in the fear of God and with loving commitment."* [10]

Fr Hillewaere was certain in his belief that The Work was a gift of God. He wrote: *"We have believed and trusted. We had to believe and trust. It was our duty".* [11] He knew, as he himself testified, of Mother Julia's *"profound spiritual life and the gifts of grace she had received, of her silent, hidden and quite simple, ordinary life, and of her down-to-earth and sensible mind".* [12]

Her gifts and graces along with his priestly commitment provided a firm basis for this new charism and for the new mandate, the development of which he was to pursue further as its spiritual father. On account of this mandate, Mother Julia would refer to him simply as 'Father', rather than 'Kapelaan' (his usual title).

This inner union with Fr Hillewaere always filled her with great happiness. A few years later, she addressed the following words to him: *"Father, it seems to me that we must work together in holy unity and complete trust, and share everything with each other. I am thinking here of the external development of The Work as well as the work of grace that our Lord allows us to participate in."* [13]

From the outset, Mother Julia referred to the charism she had received

---

[9] Letter of Mother Julia, 6 January 1980.
[10] Mother Julia's Notes, 18 January 1986.
[11] Notes of Fr Hillewaere concerning 1938.
[12] *Ibid.*
[13] Mother Julia's Notes, 24 October 1943.

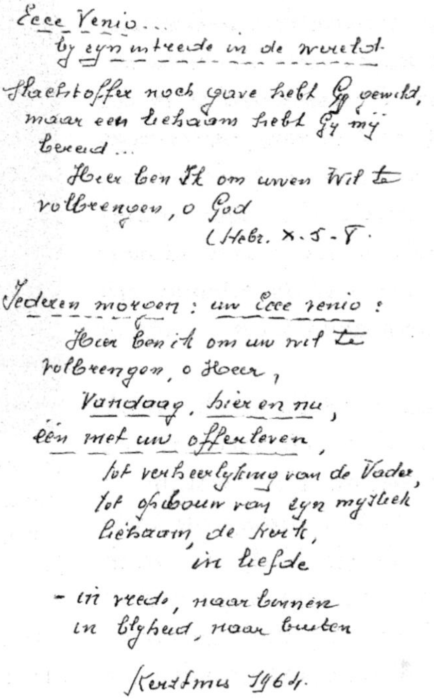

[handwritten text in Dutch:]

Ecce Venio...
by zyn intreede in de wereld.
Slachtoffer noch gave hebt Gy gewild,
maar een lichaam hebt Gy my
bereid ...
Heer ben Ik om uwen Wil te
volbrengen, o God
(Hebr. X. 5 - 8.

Iederen morgen : uw Ecce venio :
Heer ben ik om uw wil te
volbrengen, o Heer,
Vandaag, hier en nu,
één met uw offerleven,
tot verheerlyking van de Vader,
tot opbouw van zyn mystiek
lichaam, de kerk,
in liefde
- in vrede, naar binnen
in blyheid, naar buiten

Kerstmis 1964.

In the spirit of this prayer which he formulated later Fr Hillewaere surrendered himself
to God's will.

'Ecce Venio'
On coming into the world
Christ says:
'Sacrifices and offerings
you have not desired,
but a body you have prepared for me ...
    Behold I come
    to do your will, O God.'
                    (Heb 10, 5-8)

Every morning: an 'ecce venio':
    Behold I come
    to do your will, O Lord:
Here, now and today,
one with your life of sacrifice,
    to the glory of the Father,
    for the building up of the
    Mystical Body, the Church
in love,
with inner peace
and outward joy

                Christmas 1964

as The Work. She testified to its origin in this way: *"I did not consciously or deliberately seek to apply the name, The Work, to the community. Rather, I encountered it in the depths of my soul, as I became increasingly aware that the Lord was not only demanding my personal conversion, but was calling me to place myself completely and without reservation at the service of the Church, His Mystical Body, in accordance with the will of the Father."* [14]

Fr Arthur Cyriel Hillewaere, curate in Geluwe (1922-1939) and spiritual director of Mother Julia

This simple name refers to the work of Jesus Christ, of which He spoke to the Father the night before His Passion: *"I glorified you on earth by finishing the work that you gave me to do"* (Jn 17:4). His work of glorifying the Father and saving mankind continues in the Church through the power of the Holy Spirit. This name represents a call to co-operate through a generous and living faith with the mission of the Church in responding to the invitation of the Lord: *"This is the work of God, that you believe in him whom he has sent"* (Jn 6:29).

The birthday of The Work occurred at the beginning of the Week of Prayer for Christian Unity in 1938. This practice was initiated in the Anglican Communion in 1908. In 1909, Pope Pius X encouraged the participation of Catholics in the Week of Prayer, and subsequent popes laid increasing stress on the involvement of the faithful in it. [15] The heartfelt concern for greater unity could be found amongst many Christians of different denominations. This cause was always important to Mother Julia. However, she recognised that unity in its complete sense had to be rooted in the reality of everyday life, and above all within the Catholic Church. *"May they all be one"* (see Jn 17:21-23), as Jesus prayed in the Upper Room. Mother Julia wrote: *"Since 18 January 1938, the Lord has called me and others with me to live this unity in a family, to make His life and His prayer our own, and to work for Him and with Him for this unity, which in our time is so at risk. He sent us the grace of a charism to fulfil this holy vocation.*

---

[14] Mother Julia's Notes, 2 March 1994.
[15] Cf. J. LESCRAUWAET, 'Gebedsweek' in L. BRINKHOF, G.C. LAUDY, A. VERHEUL, Th.A. VISMANS, W. DE WOLF (Eds.), *Liturgische Woordenboek*, Roermond/Maaseik: J.J. Romen & Zonen 1958-1962, 796f.

He desired that it should be sealed in a 'Holy Covenant' and bound to his most Sacred Heart." [16]

In the liturgical calendar of this period, the World Week of Prayer for Christian Unity began with the feast of the Chair of Peter and ended with the feast of the Conversion of St Paul, as it still does today. These two feasts of the Apostles, that framed the Week of Prayer, made explicit the fact that faithfulness to Catholic teaching and to the successor of Peter, as well as readiness for unconditional love and a profound change of heart following St Paul's example, provides the foundation for true unity in Christ. Mother Julia saw

Mother Julia

in the complementarity of the two Apostles a luminous model for the unity and mutually supportive nature of different vocations and gifts.

Mother Julia was seized by the glory of the threefold God, which shines forth in the holiness of the Church. At the same time she was invited to make expiation for the decline of faith, for the threats to true unity, as well as for the many other wounds inflicted on the Church. This call was no longer purely private in nature, but had become a public commission for the benefit of the entire Church. Later, moved by the wonderful mystery and the supernatural beauty of the Church, Mother Julia exhorted the members of The Work: *"By our faithfulness to the grace of our vocation, may we show ourselves to be worthy sons and daughters of the Church, giving ourselves unreservedly to her service and her interests, proud of her glory and her eternal youth, courageous in our commitment and dedication, so that we may vigorously and fruitfully bear new life – for her and with her."* [17]

---

[16] Letter of Mother Julia, 12 January 1983.
[17] Mother Julia's Notes, 1971.

XII. The first developments of the charism

Mother Julia was convinced of the divine origins of the charism from the beginning: *"It is quite clear to me that The Work is God's work. He Himself has chosen the instruments, which He has destined for it. We have simply to follow His instructions. Experience shows us that God wishes to be the one who, alone, brings everything about and takes the lead."* [1]

In the weeks after 18 January 1938, Fr Hillewaere asked how God wanted the charism to progress as a concrete reality. Mother Julia gave the answer that The Work was not to be a Religious Order in the traditional sense: *"It isn't an Order. It is something quite different. It needs principles for a common life."* [2] She recognised that those called would be consecrated to God, but were to live their vocation in the world to spread the Kingdom of Christ. She wrote: *"This vocation is beautiful and to be taken seriously. Therefore the Rule will be somewhat strict. It will be found in the letters of St Paul."* [3]

She spoke of the way of life of those who were to be called – she was thinking at this time of Sisters: *"They have their own apostolic mission to fulfil in today's world and are to sacrifice themselves alongside priests. They are to be distinguished from other people through their love of God and of souls. Above all, they must strive to live the evangelical counsels, which contain everything that leads them to the most profound union with Jesus and brings them closer to souls."* [4] Mother Julia referred expressly to the fact that they had to lead a deeply spiritual life. In order to achieve this goal, they would need a comprehensive religious formation: *"Those who are called must be formed into strong and free children of God."* [5]

The time for the concrete implementation of these words had not yet arrived, as up to this point in time The Work consisted of only two people: Mother Julia and Fr Hillewaere. Together they formed the seed that over the course of the years was to grow into the communities of Sisters and Priests.

---

[1] Letters of Mother Julia, 13 and 17 August 1939.
[2] Conversation with Mother Julia, January 1938.
[3] Letters of Mother Julia, 26 February and 8 April 1938.
[4] Letter of Mother Julia, 26 February 1938.
[5] Letter of Mother Julia, 9 May 1938.

Mother Julia found refuge in Mary, whom she venerated with child-like simplicity and love. During a train journey in May 1938, she wrote the following prayer, in which she expressed her trust in the Mother of God:

> *"Dear Mother, give me your hand,*
> *guide me, that I may stand.*
> *In the unity to which I am bound*
> *like a child may I be found.*
> *Teach me to be an instrument*
> *in the Lord's saving work!*
>
> *Wherever Jesus would have me go,*
> *grant me the strength to follow*
> *His way courageously like you:*
> *Faithful in giving and serving,*
> *Steadfast and dutiful remaining*
> *With men in their mortality."* [6]

On the feast of the Sacred Heart in 1938, Mother Julia underwent another spiritual experience, which revealed to her the meaning of the 'Holy Covenant' in God's plan for the future development of The Work: *"In His light, I was able to see that the grace of the 'Holy Covenant' is intended for many others, who will give their lives to the love and mercy of God in our times. They are to be a reflection of the mystery of the Church and are to help heal the wounds that are being inflicted on the world and even on the Church through false teaching and practice."* [7]

Silently, she sought ways to develop the charism further in a spirit of integrity and readiness for service, accepting the invitation to give herself up to the Lord with even greater trust: *"I feel that He is asking me to place my trust in His almighty love unconditionally, so that I might respond to the demands He has made of me. This has increased my longing to sacrifice myself and, united with Christ, to live a life more and more hidden in God."* [8]

At the same time, she kept a look out for people, whom God might have chosen for a life of commitment to the development of The Work. Some women, who were in poor health and to whom she had given help

---

[6] Mother Julia's Notes, 20 May 1945.
[7] Mother Julia's Notes, 8 December 1985.
[8] Letter of Mother Julia, 13 January 1940.

and support, declared themselves ready to offer up their sufferings and illnesses for the new charism. Her sister, Madeleine, who was herself in poor health, was one of this group. These women were ready to sacrifice themselves and were able to understand the spirit of The Work from within, preparing the way for the first vocations.

Fr Hillewaere would occasionally speak with Canon Cardijn about The Work and the mission that this new charism could fulfil within Catholic Action. He was convinced that there ought to be consecrated people amongst the leadership of Catholic Action, contributing to its spiritual life and the renewal of its original objectives and looking after the formation of those in positions of responsibility. Canon Cardijn had a similar perspective.[9] He had already written to one of his closest colleagues, whilst convalescing in Cannes in 1919: *"Sometimes I dream of a lay Order!"* [10] In response to Fr Hillewaere's ideas, he said: *"This was my original intention."* [11] On another occasion, he added: *"I have been thinking about this problem for thirty years. I must leave it to others to take the initiative."* [12]

Shortly after the foundation of The Work, Mother Julia made the conscious decision to submit the charism that was taking shape in her heart to the approval of her bishop: *"The Work must be accepted in the heart of the Church and therefore must soon be submitted to the judgement of higher authority."* [13] In the autumn of 1938, it appeared that the time had arrived for Mother Julia to present herself to the incumbent Bishop of Bruges. On 30 September, Bishop Henry Lamiroy received Fr Hillewaere, who spoke to him about the charism of The Work. Fr Hillewaere was also in regular contact with Monsignor Mahieu, the Vicar General of the Diocese, a well-known theologian and author of numerous spiritual writings. Fr Hillewaere had been a close associate of this learned priest and would often seek and act on his guidance.

Bishop Henry Lamiroy

[9] Cf. L. ALAERTS, *Door eigen werk sterk*, pp. 182-183.
[10] M. VAN ROEY, *Cardijn*, Brussels: Reinaert 1972, p. 53.
[11] Notes of Fr Hillewaere, 1940.
[12] *Ibid.*
[13] Letter of Mother Julia, 9 July 1938.

Mother Julia was already convinced by this time that The Work had been given to the universal Church and not just to a single diocese. However, together with Fr Hillewaere, she sought to work in unison with the Bishop of Bruges and Canon Cardijn. The striving for unity arose as a response to the situation in Church and society in Belgium and in particular out of her love for the Church. This love was anchored in the charism and showed itself in her attachment to the bishop and in her concern for the spiritual renewal of Catholic Action. In Belgium, the wishes of the hierarchy concerning the apostolate in the life of the Church were so firmly embodied in the activity of Catholic Action, that new charisms, including The Work, could only develop within its sphere of influence.

With Fr Hillewaere, Mother Julia sought a way to develop the charism in this concrete situation. She wrote to her spiritual director: *"The Work is an independent foundation, a particular community and family. It has its own mission."* [14] Both she and Fr Hillewaere were of the opinion that true renewal begins with small core groups, which enlighten others through their example and their apostolic activity. At the same time, they were committed to working with Catholic Action out of love for the Church. With this in mind, she wrote to one Sister: *"When we started out, we were certainly convinced that The Work had to develop within Catholic Action and to mature into a core group. In this way we could co-operate in the mission and work of the Church. Thus, with the light of the grace of our particular vocation, we placed ourselves in the service of Catholic Action."* [15] In the same year she said once more: *"Catholic Action is a calling in the Church willed by God. Therefore, the Church must adopt its cause."* [16] Mother Julia had an unshakeable trust in the Church and at the same time was aware of the necessity of the conversion of all its members: *"Everything is founded on Christ; everything is rooted in the Church and her hierarchy. The hierarchy too is made up of men, who are in need of redemption."* [17]

In his pastoral concern not simply for priests but also for laity, Bishop Lamiroy fostered the work of Catholic Action in his diocese with all the means at his disposal. However, he wanted it to be very much a diocesan organisation and subordinate to his episcopal authority. In this he differed fundamentally with Canon Cardijn, and tension soon grew up between them. In a book on the diocese of Bruges, the author wrote: *"The Young*

---

[14] Letter of Mother Julia, 30 August 1943.
[15] Letter of Mother Julia, 19 March 1990.
[16] Letter of Mother Julia, 10 July 1948.
[17] Conversation with Mother Julia, December 1994.

Catholic Workers' organisation was above all a national movement. But Bishop Lamiroy's view was that it belonged first and foremost to the diocese. As a consequence, before the Second World War there arose a tension, which would grow even stronger after the end of the War." [18] The same book says of Bishop Lamiroy, who led the diocese of Bruges during the difficult period of 1931 to 1952 with a great sense of responsibility: *"Bishop Lamiroy always exuded an aura of gravitas, which inspired awe and respect, but did not make open dialogue easy."* [19] It was in this tense situation with its many tests of faith for Mother Julia that the charism of The Work had to develop in the following years and make its way into the future.

Mother Julia quietly hoped that Fr Hillewaere would soon be completely free to support The Work and its mission within Catholic Action. This was his wish too. At the same time her only desire was to serve God's precepts, and she wrote to her spiritual director: *"Be calm, if the bishop has other plans. We must not rush ahead of divine Providence."* [20]

In 1939 Bishop Lamiroy appointed Fr Hillewaere as parish priest of Komen-ten-Brielen, only a few kilometres from Geluwe. The faithful of Geluwe were sorry to lose their curate, because they had such a high regard for his priestly ministry. This can be seen from an obituary written by former members of Catholic Action after his death in 1972 – thirty-three years after his departure – and published in the Geluwe parish magazine: *"He was a priest with a great spirit. We knew him as a man of study, who had a feel for which trends governed our time. Like a new Paul he began the important work of formation with small groups. At the Young Catholic Worker meetings he prepared young men and women for life. Various people bear witness that Fr Hillewaere left a deep and lasting impression on them. His method involved starting with real life situations, resorting to books to master them. He had a sixth sense for which authors would leave their mark on the times. He was quiet and unassuming. He always inspired others to set out into the deep. In his time as curate he predicted that the teaching on the Mystical Body of Christ would become increasingly influential in the years to come."* [21]

Pope Pius XI died in February 1939. On 2 March, after a short conclave, Cardinal Eugenio Pacelli, the former Secretary of State, was elected as head

[18] R. BOUDENS, 'Henri Lamiroy (1931-1952)' in M. CLOET (Ed.), *Het bisdom Brugge*, Bruges: privately printed by Westvlaams Verbond van kringen voor heemkunde ²1985, p. 396.
[19] *Ibid.*, p. 395.
[20] Conversation with Mother Julia, 11 June 1939.
[21] H. DRIESSENS, 'Wij zijn samen onderweg...' in *Geluwe – Sint-Dionysius*, Weekblad, 50 (13 January 1972) 1.

Pope Pius XII

of the Catholic Church. Mother Julia saw this wise Pope of strong faith as a gift from God for such a troubled time: *"I like the Holy Father very much. He really is a holy man and so determined."* [22]

Even in this early period she experienced a spiritual longing for the recognition of The Work by Peter's successor. On 18 April 1939, she wrote:

> *"Rome stands before my eyes.*
> *The Holy Father has to give his blessing to The Work.*
> *I think that I can ask Jesus for this and strive after it."* [23]

---

[22] Conversation with Mother Julia, 30 April 1941.
[23] Letter of Mother Julia, 18 April 1939.

XIII. The start of the Second World War

Just like Mother Julia's childhood, the beginnings of The Work were overshadowed by a World War. The invasion of Poland by German armed forces on 1 September 1939 marked the start of a new war that turned a large part of Europe and then the whole world into a battlefield. The previous balance of power and political structures were overthrown. Hitler's military might terrified the population of Europe. And within a short space of time, the Nazis had succeeded in conquering several countries.[1]

The crisis, which lay behind this war, was a continuation of the problems that had led to the First World War. The effort to construct a new world order after the First World War was not sufficient to bring about a true and lasting peace between the nations. With the introduction of the Feast of Christ the King in 1925, Pope Pius XI had wanted to lead people to focus their attention on Jesus Christ. The first half of the twentieth century had already seen the widespread development of terrible ideologies, particularly Communism and Nazism. So the way was clear for the triumph of new political systems, whose ideas took hold in the minds of many, and which replaced the salvation offered by the living and true God in Jesus Christ with dangerous and worldly ideologies.

On 3 September 1939, Great Britain and France declared war on Germany. On the same day, the Belgian government declared its neutrality, but at the same time mobilised 650,000 soldiers in case the German army should try to march through Belgium.[2] In the early hours of 10 May 1940, the Nazi government in Germany ordered the start of the '*Fall Gelb*' (the 'Yellow Plan'), the 18 day long offensive from the North Sea to the southern borders of Luxembourg. In violation of their neutrality the German land and airborne divisions overran the Netherlands, Belgium and Luxembourg.[3] The defence forces were

---

[1] Cf. B. Schindler, *Chronik 1940. Tag für Tag in Wort und Bild*, Die Chronik-Bibliothek des 20. Jahrhunderts, Vol. 40, ed. by B. Harenberg, Dortmund: Chornik-Verlag ²1990, p. 7.
[2] Cf. J. Legrand, *Chronique du 20ᵉ siècle*, Paris: Chronique ²1987, p. 547.
[3] Cf. B. Schindler, *Chronik 1940*, p. 84.

mobilised immediately to oppose the invasion. Geluwe too was affected by these events.[4]

Mother Julia, who at that time was still living in the house of her deceased parents, remembered this day: *"Early in the morning French and Belgian soldiers, who had been mobilised in the night, moved in from all directions. Grief and desolation could be felt all around. I experienced this myself on my way to the early 5.30 Mass. The sky was black with aircraft. Many young men had been called up. It was an eerie sight. Mothers and children ran weeping and wailing behind the lorries filled with soldiers, who were waving flags and playing music as if they were on their way to a festival. These young, inexperienced men had all been given large quantities of alcohol, so that they would go into battle eagerly. War is so cruel and brings so much suffering with it!"* [5]

Anticipating the fall of Brussels, Canon Cardijn asked for help from Fr Hillewaere, in whom he placed great trust. Occasionally he would hide items from the archives of the Young Catholic Workers in Fr Hillewaere's presbytery in Komen-ten-Brielen. In May 1940, Canon Cardijn left Brussels with some of his closest associates. Shortly before the capture of the capital on 14 May, they arrived at Fr Hillewaere's presbytery and found refuge there.[6] In 1975, one of Canon Cardijn's colleagues recalled this event: *"In Komen-ten-Brielen we stayed with a big-hearted priest, who was a very, very good pastor to the Young Catholic Workers."* [7] Canon Cardijn and his companions remained there for four days, and then set off for Toulouse in the South of France, where at the request of the Belgian Prime Minister, they cared for the large numbers of young people, who had fled there from the Nazis on the orders of the government.[8] The leadership of the Young Catholic Workers and their co-workers ministered tirelessly to the tens of thousands of young, exhausted and undernourished refugees, who sought help in southern France.[9]

On the 25 and 26 May 1940, heavy fighting took place between Belgian and German troops in Geluwe. There were many deaths and

---

[4] Cf. D. Decuypere, *Dorp zonder grenzen*, p. 66.

[5] Mother Julia's Notes, 24 August 1992.

[6] Cf. Parish Archives Of Komen-Ten-Brielen, "Anno 1940", without page number.

[7] Archives Generales Du Royaume, "Fonds-Cardijn", Dossier No 1964/1, listed in *Inventaris van het Fonds-Cardijn*, p. 135.

[8] Cf. M. Van Roey, *Cardijn*, p. 133. Archives Generales Du Royaume, "Fonds-Cardijn", Dossier No 486, listed in *Inventaris van het Fonds-Cardijn*, p. 36.

[9] Cf. L. Alaerts, *Door eigen werk sterk,* pp. 287-293.

injuries on both sides, and a large number of Belgian soldiers were taken as prisoners of war. The civil population took shelter in the cellars of their houses during the fighting, but many still lost their lives.[10] On 28 May, King Leopold III signed the Belgian army's surrender. Belgium was to be under Nazi domination for the

Belgian war prisoners on their way to Germany at the end of May 1940

next four years.[11] At the end of May, German soldiers stormed the presbytery of Fr Hillewaere in Komen-ten-Brielen.[12] Mother Julia wrote later: *"The raid on Fr Hillewaere's presbytery in 1940 was really terrible. A group of very drunken men wanted to shoot him. How he escaped was like a miracle. Just as one of the men was loading his rifle, a German officer appeared and prevented him from shooting. In the meantime the soldiers had stolen many essential items. They remained in the presbytery for some days."* [13]

Presbytery in Komen-Ten-Brielen

A history of Geluwe in the Second World War reports that approximately two million people fled from the East into western Belgium as a result of the German army's eighteen day campaign. Hundreds of thousands of these refugees passed through Geluwe.[14] Mother Julia described these terrible events in the following words: *"People streamed into the border area from all directions,*

---

[10] Cf. D. Decuypere, *Dorp zonder grenzen*, pp. 142ff. and 211.

[11] Cf. E. Huys, *Geschiedenis van Geluwe*, p. 419. Cf. L. Alaerts, *Door eigen werk sterk*, 273ff.

[12] Cf. Parish Archives Of Komen-Ten-Brielen, "Anno 1940", without page number.

[13] Notes of Mother Julia, January 1974.

[14] Cf. D. Decuypere, *Dorp zonder grenzen*, p. 66.

*hoping to escape the violence. Many who had had to flee in panic arrived
in our village and were unable to go further. The church, the schools and
other public buildings were taken over, in order to provide accommodation
for the large numbers. Wherever there was a space on the pavements or
elsewhere, people lay down confused and exhausted. I saw and experienced
all this. My three sisters and I stayed with an elderly spinster in the village.
We did this because of my sister Madeleine's illness, and because we would
be safer in the old woman's cellar against the shelling and the attacks on the
civilian population. No words can describe the misery of war. In my soul I
understood the deeper underlying causes of this suffering and I would help,
wherever I could."* [15]

Mother Julia suffered as a result of the terrible events of the war. In
Belgium, in May 1940, 17,000 houses were destroyed, and 6,448 people
died. 22,524 were wounded and 844 went missing.[16] Amongst those
killed in action were 190 young members of the Young Catholic Workers
movement. In addition, 1,600 of them were imprisoned at the beginning
of the occupation for their commitment to their fellow countrymen in
their suffering and for their faithfulness to Christian principles.[17] Mother
Julia was shocked by the human suffering that the conflict brought with
it, in particular by the power of sin, hate and godlessness in the hearts of
so many people. She understood the devastating consequences of the war
for humanity and the Church.[18]

It was not possible for The Work to develop externally whilst the
war was going on. Once again Mother Julia found herself on a path
of unconditional faith, which she expressed in the following words:
"Everything for The Work in Christ!" [19] She possessed an inner certainty
that He would take The Work forward, and wished nothing other
than *"to be the instrument of Jesus in the sense and in the way that
He desires."* [20]

In the midst of all the danger and darkness, she knew herself to be
supported and sustained by the grace of the 'Holy Covenant': *"Jesus never
calls without providing the necessary graces. May they be accepted! I experienced
the grace of the vocation living in me in many circumstances, but particularly*

---

[15] Mother Julia's Notes, 24 August 1992.
[16] Cf. L. ALAERTS, *Door eigen werk sterk,* p. 295.
[17] Cf. *ibid.*, p. 287ff.
[18] Cf. C. HÜNERMANN, *Chronik 1941. Tag für Tag in Wort und Bild*, Die Chronik Bibliothek des 20. Jahrhundert, Vol 41, ed. by B. Harenberg, Gütersloh-München: Chronik im Bertelsmann Lexikon Verlag 2001, p. 20.
[19] Letter of Mother Julia, 29 August 1940.
[20] Letter of Mother Julia, August 1940.

in hours of trial. This time was for me also a time of deep purification in every sense. God strengthened me, and the light of the grace of my vocation which surrounded me gave me the power to go on and to answer the call that Christ had placed in me through the commitment to the 'Holy Covenant'. " [21]

---

[21] *Ibid.*; Mother Julia's Notes, 24 August 1992.

XIV. Leaving her parents' home

Mother Julia thought for a long time about whether she should leave her parents' house for the sake of the charism. She had already considered this course of action and spoken to Fr Hillewaere about it as early as 1938. On his advice she was to remain there for another three years. The hour God had chosen for her departure from the parental home had not yet arrived. Obedience to her spiritual companion was her guarantee that she was on the right path: *"For me, being obedient means acting and living in secure freedom."* [1]

In July 1941, she became convinced that she ought to leave her parents' house, just as Abraham had left his homeland behind him at God's call. She asked Fr Hillewaere for his consent. Whilst making her aware of the risk she was taking, he answered her request, *"Do what God has placed in your heart!"*,[2] and blessed her. He knew how strong in faith and down to earth she was. *"I now realise,"* she was to say later, *"that God was leading The Work forward, as I left my parents' house."* [3] For some time she had known that the situation at home no longer provided the necessary conditions for the development of the charism. The future contained no worldly security, and it was no easy matter, leaving her ill sister, with whom she would often speak about The Work and the concerns of the Church: *"Madeleine, my dear sister, was very ill; our souls were bound together by a deep affinity."* [4] Madeleine would gladly have moved away from home with Mother Julia, but because of her heart condition she could not even consider such a move. Instead, she readily offered up her illness for the growth of the charism.

Madeleine, Mother Julia's sister

---

[1] Letter of Mother Julia, 21 November 1939.
[2] Conversation with Mother Julia, written down 5 August 1989.
[3] Conversation with Mother Julia, 1 February 1997.
[4] *Ibid.*

The war could not prevent Mother Julia following the Lord's call: *"'Forget your people and your father's house!' (Ps 45:11) – 'Follow me!' (Jn 1:43). Jesus's thirst for souls had penetrated me deeply and I was ready to sacrifice myself. Through all this there resounded in my soul the hymn: 'Nearer, my God, to Thee'."* [5] On 16 July 1941, in the middle of the war, whilst in poor health, without a profession, without work and without human security, she left her parents' house and her sisters, who still lived there. She knew herself to be under the guidance of Our Lady of Mount Carmel, whose memorial was celebrated on this day. She wrote later: *"Full of faith, I placed my hand in that of the Mother of Carmel. She held me fast and helped me fulfil the will of God throughout the remaining war years. 'Magnificat anima mea Dominum!' – 'My soul glorifies the Lord!' Mary was my only security in the present and for the future, which was known to God alone. It seemed to me that she, our Mother, had taken responsibility for my life, and carried me on day by day."* [6]

Mother Julia obeyed the call of the Lord in love and set out on a pilgrimage of faith. The 'Holy Covenant' helped her to preserve a spirit of serenity. She knew that she was sustained by God's grace, with which she had chosen to co-operate by a free and generous decision: *"Grace does not work automatically. It does not force itself on you. To God's Church and people, it is a gift of His inexhaustible Mercy and infinite Goodness for the salvation and healing of many. Grace is enveloped in and filled by the law of divine love, and hence places demands according to its nature. Thus, I was able to get to know grace, seeing it, experiencing it and living it, in a faith that united what was put asunder, healed what was wounded and sick, and caused what was unfruitful to bear fruit."* [7]

Mother Julia recognised that with this Yes to God's call she was being allowed to anticipate the Yes of her future Sisters and Brothers. Her faithful commitment was to find an echo in the lives of many people. Looking back on this day, she wrote many years later to the members of The Work: *"When I began my pilgrimage under the protection of the Mother of Carmel, it was God's will and decree that hidden and implicit in the single Yes I gave to Him was the Yes of each of you. Never forget this, for your Yes too contains in it the call to the same pilgrimage, which you have to follow through this time, through this now, which makes up the story of your life."* [8]

[5] Mother Julia's Notes, 24 August 1992.
[6] *Ibid.*; Letter of Mother Julia, 16 July 1981.
[7] Mother Julia's Notes, 1974.
[8] Circular Letter of Mother Julia, August 1976.

Where did Mother Julia go, when she left Geluwe? Initially, she travelled to Kortrijk, where she found accommodation in Bethany, the retreat house of the Sisters of St Vincent de Paul. Shortly afterwards, through an acquaintance, she obtained a position with a family in Sint-Niklaas, which was more than ninety kilometres from Geluwe.

Here Mother Julia soon won the trust of her employers, who were intelligent and open-minded. They conversed with her frequently and regarded her as a very well educated woman, who – so they thought – must have undertaken advanced studies. They were astonished when they heard that in reality she had had only the most basic education. Although surprised by it, they respected her need to go to Mass every morning. It was a long way to the parish church. Mother Julia remembered: *"The house was very isolated. I persevered through frost, cold and darkness. The Mass was my mainstay. I used to get up very early."* [9] The parish priest was impressed by this young woman's readiness for sacrifice. He was very happy to open up the Church half an hour earlier for her and for a girl whom she had come to know and with whom she had developed a spiritual friendship.

The woman with whom Mother Julia had found work soon realised that her health was poor. So she decided to do the heavier housework herself and to hand over much of the responsibility for the upbringing of her four children to her employee. The children loved Mother Julia and were happy to be with her. She appreciated the goodwill of her employer, but her conscience became troubled. For she was convinced that she ought not to take the place of the mother, who had the primary responsibility for the upbringing of the children.

This issue of conscience, combined with the difficult situations arising from the war, persuaded Mother Julia to seek another position. The employer, a sensitive woman, sensed something of her vocation, and therefore before she left the family offered to help her obtain possible entry into a Carmel. She had learnt that Mother Julia belonged to the Carmelite Third Order Secular and had allowed her to attend the monthly meetings. Mother Julia, however, was aware that God had a different plan for her.

Whilst the Second World War raged and she could not foresee the concrete development of The Work, the nature of the charism became increasingly clear to her. She declared in November 1941: *"It seems to me that the good God has made me stronger and stronger in all that constitutes*

---

[9] Conversation with Mother Julia, 5 August 1989.

The Work. God's Word, which I heard in the stillness of my heart, is being fulfilled." [10]

The 16 July always remained for Mother Julia a day of thanksgiving and wonder at the marvellous ways of divine Providence. Many years later, as, once again, that date drew closer, she wrote: *"As I prepare for the blessed anniversary of the day on which the Mother of Carmel majestically took me in hand, in order to lead me further on the way of The Work of Jesus, my heart overflows with thanksgiving, peace and deep joy. Like a child to its mother, I gave myself over to her at that time, and entrusted to her my entire future, which was still unknown to me. She has taught me above all else to understand and to live genuine trust, which, it seems to me, is the courage to remain faithful in every trial. It is like the faithfulness of the bride, who believes in the faithfulness of her bridegroom."* [11]

---

[10] Letter of Mother Julia, 21 November 1941.
[11] Letter of Mother Julia, 11 July 1978.

XV. With young women in domestic service

In October 1941, Fr Berthold, a respected Carmelite priest, recommended to Mother Julia a new position in Kortrijk. She took over the running of the household of a wealthy woman, who owned two dogs and a parrot. Mother Julia was so irritated by the peculiar atmosphere in the house that for a week she did not unpack her bags. However, in the end she decided to remain because she believed strongly that God's Providence had led her there.

Mother Julia in Kortrijk

Whilst attending Mass, she met a young woman, who cared for the many domestic maids who were employed in families in Kortrijk. It was uncommon at that time in Flanders for young women to learn a profession or to study. Many were employed in domestic service and childcare, whilst others worked in factories and workshops. A large number of the domestic maids in Kortrijk belonged to a branch of the Young Catholic Workers. After a few months, the woman responsible for the group asked Mother Julia for help in its running, and shortly afterwards she took over responsibility for it completely. So it came about naturally that Mother Julia was given the opportunity to support others in their faith. Although she did not belong to Catholic Action and had reservations about some of its developments, she readily accepted this task in obedience. Fr Hillewaere had asked her to take on this apostolic work assisting the young.

The new position demanded all Mother Julia's strength. Once again she was responsible for the entire household. Because she was conscientious in her work and carried it out willingly, her employer soon developed a trust and affection for her, giving her permission to care for the domestic maids in Kortrijk in her free time. Alongside her motherly concern for the young women, Mother Julia endeavoured to help her employer grow in the faith: *"I want to lead the lady to a more noble life. This demands empathy, sacrifice and a complete forgetfulness of self. May she discover, experience and know God in her life, how good He is and how much He loves us."* [1]

Also employed in the household was a young man, named Vincent, who was grateful for having been given refuge there in the chaos of the war.[2] He came from a good, large family and was a great help to Mother Julia. He would often give her the addresses of young women with whom he was acquainted. Whilst out walking the dogs, he would undertake errands for Mother Julia, including delivery of the letters she had written to the maids. She too would have to take the dogs out occasionally, and this provided her with the opportunity to meet up with different families and young women. In later years she recalled: *"I got to know many servant girls through Vincent. My employer introduced me to the social world of Kortrijk. This proved very useful in giving me access to domestic staff and to good families who were looking for young women to go into service."* [3] Mother Julia was always alert to the opportunity to use these situations for the benefit of the kingdom of God, and very quickly gathered a large circle of young women around her.

The thirty-one year old Mother Julia received particular support from Fr Berthold, who lived in a monastery close to her place of work. Fr Berthold understood the need to combine ascetic rigour and open-heartedness,

contemplative silence and apostolic zeal. He was a man of God, who possessed a strong priestly charisma, and was a much sought-after confessor and preacher of days of recollection and retreats. His writings on Carmelite spirituality were very influential.[4] He sensed that Mother Julia was deeply contemplative and burned with an inner fire to win souls for God.

In her work with the young women employed in domestic service, Mother Julia was supported by several group leaders. She was concerned that they

Fr Berthold of Jesus, OCD

---

[1] Letter of Mother Julia, 5 August 1942.
[2] Cf. L. ALAERTS, *Door eigen werk sterk*, pp. 321-324.
[3] Mother Julia's Notes, 13 April 1991.
[4] Cf. Discalced Carmelites, Archives of the Province, Carmel Ghent.

should deepen their unity in faith with Jesus and with each other, and should nurture a sense of responsibility. She would circulate a weekly letter among them, in order to encourage them in their commitment to the Church and to prepare them for their future lives. She would sometimes show these letters to Fr Berthold and ask him

The Carmelite church in Kortrijk

to go through them and improve them. The concern to work alongside priests and to live in a way that was mutually complementary with them was close to Mother Julia's heart. This had an increasingly important place in the charism. She wrote at the time: *"Fr Berthold is very devoted to our Work. He keeps a wise eye on everything. From time to time I send him the weekly circular letter."* [5]

Some of these circular letters have been preserved. They witness to the joyful spirit of faith that Mother Julia possessed and that allowed her to help young people to cope in faith with their often difficult daily lives. She succeeded in illuminating the lives of the young women with the ideal of a profound love of Christ and joy at the word of God: *"How the words of our divine Teacher in the Gospel must speak to us! How they must enthuse us in our gatherings and in the fulfilment of our tasks!"* [6] She referred time and time again to the wonderful mystery of the Church: *"It is wonderful for us to be allowed to participate in the life of the Church. Have we considered this and appreciated it sufficiently up to now? We must become – now or never – young women, who can live and radiate what we have received from Christ through the Church, and who wish to pass it on."* [7]

She asked the young servant girls to give support to priests in their mission and to treat their vocation with great respect. She encouraged them to remain faithful to Canon Cardijn. In 1942, in the difficult situation created by the German occupation, he called on young workers to commit themselves fearlessly to Christian principles: *"We are faced with*

[5] Letter of Mother Julia, 9 August 1942.
[6] Circular Letter of Mother Julia to the domestic maids, 8 July 1942.
[7] Circular Letter of Mother Julia to the domestic maids, 10 June 1942.

two opposed and irreconcilable tendencies in the education of the young, on one side a pagan and on the other a personal, Christian direction. We must accept the setbacks and trials of the war as opportunities, offered to us by Providence, to bear unshakeable witness to our faith in the personal worth and the temporal and eternal end of the young workers. We must be the first Christians of the new era." [8] After he was jailed for a few months in the prison of St Giles in Brussels on account of this speech,[9] Mother Julia wrote to the young women: *"We sympathise with him in his loneliness. No walls or distance can let us forget what he has achieved for young workers. Through the sacrifice of our service and of our apostolic dedication we unite ourselves with his selfless sacrifice. We both pray for his release and submit ourselves to God's Providence."* [10]

Mother Julia was an educator. She awakened in the maids, who had little social standing, the consciousness of their value as women, as baptised members of the Church, leading them to a life of virtue and spirituality. She opposed decisively any lack of commitment, placing great value on the idea that no-one should miss the common worship and meetings without good reason, and that everyone should pay their membership contributions on time. At the same time she made it clear to the maids, who had little knowledge of the law, that they were personally responsible for knowing the laws that affected their work and for applying them with a Christian conscience. She worked to form their characters and devised concrete resolutions for them to apply in their daily lives. In order to receive God's blessing on the retreat for the leaders of Catholic Action, she made the following invocation: *"On 20 May we offer up our communal Mass in sisterly unity, and ask the Holy Spirit to send the Church good leaders and to fill them with his seven gifts."* [11]

One of her main concerns was to help the maids to make the right decisions concerning their lives and to prepare them for the future. She asked the following questions: *"Have we ever thought seriously about the direction in which our lives as young women are going? Have we considered that for each woman God has decreed eternally a particular way and state of life? From your youth onwards you must go towards a future, in which you develop from a girl into a woman, whether you choose to marry or to enter the religious life. In us and in every young woman, God's plan manifests itself in*

---

[8] J. CARDIJN, *Jeunes travailleurs face aux temps nouveaux*, Brussels: Editions Jocistes 1942, pp. 18-19.
[9] Cf. M. FIEVEZ and J. MEERT, *Cardijn*, p. 144; L. ALAERTS, *Door eigen werk sterk*, p. 312.
[10] Circular Letter of Mother Julia to the domestic maids, 1 July 1942.
[11] Circular Letter of Mother Julia to the domestic maids, 25 May 1942.

a completely personal way, in the dispositions of heart and temperament, as they are revealed and develop over the course of the years according to God's summons and call." [12]

Mother Julia wanted to form women of fully human, as well as religious, maturity. She felt that many of the maids could not properly develop their personalities in the often difficult circumstances in which they worked. Therefore she was very keen to provide assistance to them in growing to maturity in thought, sensitivity and will. Her priority was not great numbers. She gave the maids a sense of security and showed empathy and realism in preparing them for the demands of life. After a few weeks, she was able to note with joy, a new spirit had begun to show itself in the group. She loved them with all her heart and wrote to Fr Hillewaere: *"I get so much from seeing the girls."* [13] Canon Cardijn also expressed his esteem for the apostolate in Kortrijk and at a meeting in Brussels said to the leader, through whom Mother Julia had become involved in working with the maids: *"All my good wishes! Say to all the leaders that I bless them and that they should persevere in the great and beautiful work they have begun. Such people must lead the female branch of the Young Workers."* [14]

Several of the principal members of Catholic Action were both astonished at and thankful for Mother Julia's activities. Others, however, possessed little understanding of what she was doing, for she had her own particular focus. She was not so much interested in external activities, but rather in the deepening of faith and the formation of conscience. She was primarily concerned with purity of intention, with true joy in living, and the striving for a holiness that could prove itself genuine and credible in all situations. External actions would arise out of such efforts and become a pure and joyful service. She had learnt this from St Paul, who wrote to his pupil Timothy: *"Fight the good fight, faithfully and with a good conscience"* (1 Tim 1:19). In her work with the maids she showed how, in practice, the charism of The Work ought to be lived in apostolic service and which principles were to be considered important.

Mother Julia followed her own path in her work with the young, and, although difficulties in working together could not be avoided, was sincerely concerned to maintain unity with the leadership of Catholic Action in Kortrijk. In a letter, she wrote: *"It is impossible for me to do on my*

---

[12] Circular Letter of Mother Julia to the domestic maids, 5 August 1942.
[13] Letter of Mother Julia, 9 August 1942.
[14] Quoted in a letter to the domestic maids, also to Mother Julia, 1942.

Some of the girls who were accompanied in their lives by Mother Julia

own, what must be accomplished together."[15] The struggle for unity was always close to her heart.

At the end of September 1942, Mother Julia left Kortrijk. Her employer, who had begun a journey of conversion under her positive influence and had grown very fond of her, was upset about her departure. According to Mother Julia: *"She simply cannot grasp or accept it; she is trying to get me to stay with her by every means possible."* [16]

With her departure the time had also come to hand over responsibility for the care of the maids to others. Mother Julia reported in a letter: *"All our maids came; they were sad because they had to take their leave of me. In this parting I experienced, how much I had lived and worked for them, and how I bore them and the whole undertaking in my heart."* [17]

Why did Mother Julia leave? She had come to recognise in her conscience that this separation was necessary because of the difficulties she was encountering with the leadership of the Young Catholic Women in Kortrijk: *"More than ever I feel that I cannot operate within the confines of this group in its current stage of development. I thank the Lord for what I was able to experience in Kortrijk."* [18] It became clearer to her that she had to reduce her occupational and apostolic obligations and be more available for the further development of The Work. *"In my thinking"*, she wrote to Fr Hillewaere, *"I am drawn more and more to the heart of The Work. By the heart of The Work I mean its foundation. I offer my life to God constantly and without condition, so that His Work may develop further."* [19] In addition,

---

[15] Letter of Mother Julia, 30 July 1942.
[16] Letter of Mother Julia, 27 September 1942.
[17] Letter of Mother Julia, 4 October 1942.
[18] Letter of Mother Julia, 17 October 1942.
[19] Letter of Mother Julia, 20 July 1942.

her sister was badly in need of assistance, as her health had worsened. With Fr Hillewaere's agreement Mother Julia returned to Geluwe for a short time, in order to look after Madeleine, who was called to her eternal rest a few months later. There was a spiritual bond between them and Mother Julia was at her side as she died. She remained ever thankful to her sister for having given her life and suffering to the Lord for the development of The Work. In spite of the love and high regard she had for her sisters, her temporary return to Geluwe was bound up with sacrifice and renunciation: *"I must adapt to so many situations which are foreign to me and do not correspond to my intentions."* [20]

Mother Julia remained in contact with several women from Kortrijk during her stay in Geluwe. From one of the letters she received we can see what influence she had on the young: *"I felt that our Movement would progress well as long as you were involved in it. By that I mean in particular the development of the spiritual, which is so necessary and is being neglected once more."* [21] Another woman, whom she had helped to find her vocation to the consecrated life, wrote to her, *"I would like to thank you very much for your letter and for your prayers. They were very welcome. I have no spiritual director. Can you help me? I would like to progress in the interior life and am still so weak that I need support."* [22] Several years later Mother Julia visited some of the maids who had married in the meantime. She wrote of this visit: *"I thank Jesus for the good that He continues to work in these young women. I believe I can say that every one of them tries in her own way to be a good mother and to build up her family with Christian principles."* [23]

Fr Berthold too spoke very positively of Mother Julia's apostolic influence amongst the young women of Kortrijk. He offered her his priestly support and assured her that he considered her work amongst the maids *"a thing of God"*.[24]

---

[20] Letter of Mother Julia, 30 October 1942.
[21] Letter to Mother Julia, 8 November 1942.
[22] Letter to Mother Julia, August 1942.
[23] Letter of Mother Julia, 25 November 1948.
[24] Quoted in a letter of Mother Julia, 27 September 1942.

XVI. Concern for unity

On 29 June 1943, Pope Pius XII published the encyclical, 'Mystici Corporis Christi', in which he set out in a striking manner the mystery of the Church, and called the faithful to a deeper unity with Christ, the Head of the Church, and with each other. At the beginning of the encyclical we read: *"We intend to speak of the riches stored up in this Church, which Christ purchased with His own Blood, and whose members glory in a Head crowned with thorns."*[1] Elsewhere in the encyclical, the Pope writes: *"Our pastoral office now requires that we provide an incentive for the heart to love this Mystical Body with that spiritual love, which is not confined to thoughts and words but expresses itself in deeds."*[2] Pius XII stated his wish that all the members of the Church should collaborate in her apostolic mission. In this regard he praised the members of Catholic Action who assisted the clergy in their apostolic labours. He also recognised the role of other Associations, seeing clearly the importance of the involvement of all in the Church's mission, particularly given the circumstances of the time.[3]

Mother Julia rejoiced at this papal letter and saw in it an official acknowledgement of the mission that she had carried in her heart for many years and that was taking shape in the charism of The Work. She shared his organic view of the Church, in which faithfulness to the hierarchy was coupled with mutually compatible charisms and gifts. Fr Hillewaere, who for years had placed an understanding of the Church as the Mystical Body of Christ at the centre of his priestly work,[4] also regarded the encyclical as a great gift.

During this period, Mother Julia passed some months in Brussels with the consent of Fr Hillewaere and the agreement of Bishop Lamiroy, in order to spend time discerning more precisely God's plan for The Work. She wrote: *"I am firmly convinced that the Lord takes the lead in*

---

[1] Pope Pius XII, *The Mystical Body of Christ*, Catholic Truth Society, London 1943, para. 2.
[2] *Ibid.*, para. 91.
[3] Cf. *Ibid.*, para. 98 ff.
[4] Cf. H. DRIESSENS, *Wij zijn samen onderweg...*, in: *Geluwe – Sint Dionysius*, Weekblad, 50 (13 January 1972) 1.

everything and makes use of concrete circumstances. I shall always endeavour to remain dependent on God's Spirit and to regulate my activity, so that nothing the Lord has entrusted me with is obstructed or undermined. My care and commitment are entirely for those who are called to The Work. I have not yet discerned the Lord's concrete plans, but I am convinced that, when the moment determined by Providence arrives, He will not keep them hidden from me." [5]

In Brussels she experienced new initiatives in the Church. She rejoiced at these, but was also concerned about the lack of unity and collaboration between them. She constantly asked herself how the charism she had been sent could assist the different organisations and movements in recognising

their mutually complementary natures: *"I have an increasingly strong yearning, through everything I am and strive to do, to contribute to greater unity amongst the children of the Church of God."* [6] Mother Julia was aware that the gift of grace entrusted to her was a far-reaching charism of unity.

Grand-Place, Brussels

She considered that this unity included the harmonious coexistence of the apostolic and contemplative lives. Fr Hillewaere shared this conviction, which had become very important to him in his priestly ministry and through his studies. In view of his concerns over developments occurring in some Church groups he declared: *"There has to be a unity between the contemplative life and the apostolic mission. The active apostolate must be ordered in such a way that it not only does not damage the spiritual life, but actually encourages contemplation!"* [7]

Mother Julia's personality attracted attention in Brussels as a result of various encounters. *"She is exceptionally down-to-earth and alert, and is not easily influenced by others"*,[8] said one young woman. A female academic, who taught biblical studies, stated: *"I think that someone with an intellect*

[5] Letter of Mother Julia, 20 September 1943.
[6] Letter of Mother Julia, 28 September 1943.
[7] Notes of Fr Hillewaere, 1 December 1942.
[8] Quoted in a letter of Mother Julia, 5 June 1944.

such as Julia's has to be introduced into scholarly circles!" [9] Nor did her wide knowledge and profound understanding of Holy Scripture remain hidden. One day she was asked some questions which she answered in the following way: What books are you interested in? – *"The Gospels."* – How do you

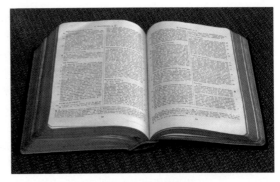

French Bible used by Mother Julia

make them your own? – *"I seek the truth of Christ's teaching in them and try to live my life accordingly."* – How did you come to have such a deep grasp of the Gospels? – *"I can't explain that; one should strive for the truth."* [10]

From the pure spring of the Gospel she drew that wisdom that the world cannot give. She emphasised the need for every apostolic activity to be rooted in the truth of the Gospels: *"One must recognise all of the truth that comes from God."* [11] In her burning love for the mystical body of Christ she was convinced that there should exist a loving unity, a sincere collaboration, and a fruitful complementarity amongst the faithful who participate in the apostolic mission of the Church. She pointed out that the same apostolic work unites all the different organisations: *"I see no difference between the various forms of the apostolate. The apostolate is an outpouring and overflowing of God's grace into the soul and a further pouring of grace from soul to soul."* [12]

With the same conviction she emphasised that every work of God had to fulfil its particular mission in the Body of the Church and had to remain faithful to its own ends. It requires great powers of discernment to recognise, alongside that which all Church organisations share, what is peculiar to a charism, and to be able to distinguish the authentic from the inauthentic, and selfless dedication to the Church from the concern for worldly advancement. As she declared on one occasion: *"Anyone who gives himself over to illusions cannot rejoice in the truth. It is a matter of co-operating with grace. We work for the honour of God. We do not work in order*

[9] Notes of Fr Hillewaere, 3 January 1944.
[10] Account in a letter of Mother Julia, 16 January 1944.
[11] Notes of Fr Hillewaere, 3 January 1944.
[12] Conversation with Mother Julia, 15 March 1980.

to shine before others through our work, but so that the glory of God can shine forth. As soon as we seek our own honour and our own esteem, we place unity in danger. In place of true accord, we find great conflict!" [13]

In one letter she wrote of two important apostolic works within the Church: *"I understand very well that both works are distinct in their goals and in their spheres of action. But it seems to me that the Lord, who has given life to both of them, has also given them the necessary means to develop fully so that they will work together with real understanding of each other and speak as one voice, strengthening unity for the good of the Church. They should not make life impossible for each other, but complement and enrich each other. The wise Providence of God has entrusted each work with its own mission. And since both works have been founded to respond to a new need in the Church, it is important that they join forces to withstand the attacks of the enemy."* [14]

Just as Christ served the apostles, the various works of God are to serve the Church and each other: *"Is it not necessary that our participation in the saving love of Christ should widen our perspective, so that we can see both works with His eyes? It has just come to my mind that Our Lord did not find it beneath His dignity to serve the apostles and to wash their feet. I am surprised that one organisation would not wish to work together with others."* [15]

Mother Julia was of the opinion that individual charisms ought not to consider just themselves, but should seek to co-operate with other organisations out of love for the Church. She said, in her clear and simple manner: *"Unity must first be achieved between them before they can become effective. There is only one calling, and that is love. The various charisms are channels through which God pours out his mercy in various ways and permits it to flow into the Church, so that she might be a great power and serve the ends willed by God."* [16] She possessed a yearning for the collaboration of all the positive forces in the Church and in society and for a real renewal in truth, justice and love: *"I am especially happy to know that there are many sons and daughters of the Church striving for unity in the love of Christ. Unity is my whole desire. There lives in me a great and powerful longing: that Christ should be loved."* [17]

---

[13] Letter of Mother Julia, 6 May 1944. Conversation with Mother Julia, 21 February 1994.
[14] Letter of Mother Julia, 28 September 1943.
[15] *Ibid.*
[16] Letter of Mother Julia, 10 December 1941. Conversation with Mother Julia, April 1993.
[17] Letters of Mother Julia, 5 August 1942 and 20 September 1943.

In order to build up and strengthen unity, Mother Julia not only participated in many conversations, but also constantly offered up to the Lord her readiness for sacrifice, her prayer and her suffering as expiation. Not everyone was able to understand her striving for unity. But, in spite of tensions and difficulties, she experienced a deep, inner happiness. She wrote to Fr Hillewaere: *"In God's light I have been able to discern that all this glorifies Him. This gives me such inner joy that I cannot express it in words. It seems to me that for a moment I am suffused with the beatitude of those who are persecuted for the sake of righteousness."* [18]

Whilst she promoted unity between different charisms, the war continued to rage, creating new barriers between nations. With her gift of discernment, she was able to grasp clearly the widespread spiritual trends of the day – such as individualism, liberalism, communism, materialism – and their effects on people's thinking, feeling and acting. She was always concerned to respond to such trends in the light of faith: *"In this light my mind watches out for authentic renewal and evangelisation, which is sustained by prayer and penance, by expiation and a turning away from sin. It is in this way that a conversion and turning to the commandments of God in faith and commitment to Jesus Christ becomes possible."* [19]

---

[18] Letter of Mother Julia, 10 July 1944.
[19] Mother Julia's Notes, 24 August 1992.

THIRD PART

Beginning of a Common Life
(1944-1950)

XVII. The first vocations

In July 1944, Mother Julia became ill and returned to Geluwe from Brussels. She was forced to spend some months in her deceased parents' house on account of her poor health. Fr Berthold tried to get her to go back to Kortrijk, with the intention of getting her a job as a portress with the Carmelites, thus allowing her to continue working with young women in domestic service. However, this did not prove possible as Kortrijk had been heavily bombed. More than 600 people had been killed there between 9 October 1942 and 21 July 1944. In one family that Mother Julia knew well, six of the twelve children lost their lives. More than 1,800 buildings were completely destroyed.[1]

Fr Berthold recognised Mother Julia's contemplative vocation and had hoped that one day she would enter the Carmel. Gradually, however, he began to sense that God was calling her to something else. *"Julia, for a long time I seriously thought that, as a fervent member of the Third Order, you would one day find your way into the Carmel. But now I am convinced that you have a special vocation to something quite different."* [2]

Even as Mother Julia continued to experience her powerlessness to realise her vocation, she knew she was sustained by God's power and accompanied by Saint Paul: *"With Saint Paul, my beloved brother in heaven, I can do nothing other than confess: When the Lord sends a soul the highest gift of Himself, this transcends all words and thoughts and cannot be compared with anything else."* [3]

God ordained that from the beginning through Mother Julia and Fr Hillewaere, He would lay the foundations for the communities of Sisters and Priests. The first concrete steps were directed at the development of a community of consecrated women. For several years now, Mother Julia had been in contact with some young people, who were attracted to the charism she had received. These women sensed the presence of God in her and were thankful for the spiritual guidance she gave them. Mother Julia commented on this in a letter she sent to Fr Hillewaere: *"It is not necessary for the young people to thank me, for having brought a ray of light into their*

---

[1] Cf. D. DECUYPERE, *Dorp zonder grenzen*, pp. 378-379.
[2] Quoted in a letter of Mother Julia, 17 September 1943.
[3] Letter of Mother Julia, 29 October 1944.

lives. This certainly did not come from me. I am amazed at it myself. It is the Lord, who makes use of me to send them these sparks of light and this joy. To Him alone are thanks due. I have done no more than my duty." [4] Mother Julia had composed a 'small rule' for these women, to help them to recognise and love the spirit of their vocation.

By this time she had formulated a clear idea of how their fellowship in the spirit of the charism could be strengthened: *"I believe that it is a good thing that those who are called should foster a spontaneous warmth towards each other. They should develop a family spirit and nurture the development of community. By that, I mean that those who have chosen this vocation and are already bound to each other in the Holy Spirit, should work together enthusiastically in unity, with magnanimous readiness for sacrifice and self-renunciation for the realisation of The Work, to the extent and in the manner ordained by divine Providence."* [5]

Mother Julia invited the initial group of those called to come together once a month to think about and discuss a point from the 'small rule'. When this was not possible because of the difficulties created for the Church by the war,[6] they remained in contact by letter and would set aside a day, on which they would keep a day of retreat, each in her own place. Physical distance was to be overcome by this spiritual bond. Mother Julia continually pointed out that true unity must be rooted in the Sacrament of the Eucharist, and had for a long time been in the habit of praying for unity after the reception of Holy Communion.

After a period of preparation, the young women, who were gradually moving towards the consecrated life in The Work, entered into the 'Holy Covenant' with the Heart of Jesus. In this way they participated in the special gifts of grace that had been given to Mother Julia in 1934. They soon found that the 'Holy Covenant' not only bound them more deeply to Jesus Christ, but also welded them together as a family of God. One of them wrote: *"The community spirit is growing beautifully, because we are united together by the 'Covenant'."* [7]

Mother Julia bore the following testimony to the unifying power of the 'Holy Covenant': *"I strive to fulfil my mission and duty and every day to live my 'Holy Covenant' with the family of The Work completely. Since the covenant has taken on a more profound dimension, it seems to me that as each day passes*

---

[4] Letter of Mother Julia, 2 October 1943.
[5] Letter of Mother Julia, 20 July 1943.
[6] Cf. L. ALAERTS, *Door eigen werk sterk*, p. 319ff.
[7] Quoted in a letter of Mother Julia, 30 August 1943.

I bear ever more in my heart those who are called." [8]

The 'Holy Covenant' strengthened those called in their commitment to the spiritual renewal of the Church, particularly in their work amongst the female branch of the Young Catholic Workers. Mother Julia wrote of this: *"The Lord brought the first vocations together in unity and awoke in them the power of life lived in the hidden greatness of His love. Since then He has never ceased to draw and lead them on, and to unite them in the 'Holy Covenant' that they have taken up with each other. The 'Holy Covenant' entails that those called should be one in heart and soul for the sake of the Church, that they grow in the spirit of their vocation and consecrate themselves to the things of the Lord, so that The Work may continue to develop. For the sake of*

Some of the first vocations

the Church, The Work must forge an inviolable family bond from which new forces of life will pour forth into the Church." [9] The members were to live their vocation in the unity of a family of God and to serve the Church with joyful hearts.

Fr Hillewaere, who had been the parish priest in Menin since 4 March 1943, supported and provided them with direction. The mutual assistance they gave each other in the grace of the 'Holy Covenant' was a source of strength and helped those who were called to recognise the signs of the times and to respond to them in a spirit of discernment. Conscious of the magnitude of this grace, Mother Julia declared to Fr Hillewaere: *"Through everything I experience a spiritual happiness in living up to the 'Holy Covenant'. Father, may I ask that you often remind those called to The Work of their 'Holy Covenant', so that, whatever the difficulties, they may grow in the spirit of their vocation! Make them aware that in living up to the 'Holy Covenant' they receive all the graces they need, all the graces that the Lord has placed in the 'Holy Covenant'."* [10]

---

[8] Letters of Mother Julia, 2 October and 5 December 1943.
[9] Letter of Mother Julia, 26 February 1944.
[10] Letter of Mother Julia, 12 February 1944.

On 30 November 1944, Mother Julia travelled from Geluwe to Sint-Niklaas, to assist a member of the group, whose father had been paralysed by a stroke and whose mother was very ill. She was accepted like a daughter into this family, and had the opportunity to provide support and direction to some young women in Sint-Niklaas, who were associated with The Work, and were employed as teachers, office workers, and in various domestic activities, as well as being actively involved with the young. Some of them were even asked to take on senior leadership roles in Catholic Action. In their apostolic commitment they strove to be united with Mother Julia, Fr Hillewaere and Canon Cardijn.

After some time, Mother Julia decided to look for another position. The care of the young woman's parents had become too demanding on her time and strength, and she felt the need to be freer to serve the Lord, to develop The Work and to assist those called to it. She wrote to Fr Hillewaere: *"I think it is time for me to remove myself from this situation. I long to give myself more to Jesus and to souls. Father, ought I not rather to remain in Sint-Niklaas and work in a factory to earn my living? How will that affect my health? I believe that Jesus will help me. In Him I find the strength and the joy in living that I need to choose the best part or, to express it better, to choose Him."* [11]

On 1 June 1945 she started working in a textile and hosiery mill in Sint-Niklaas, sharing digs in a widow's house with another young woman called to The Work, and experiencing how the charism could be lived in the workplace. She worked in the mill for three months, and described her experience thus: *"Between 300 and 500 men and women worked for the company. Sometimes, the post war situation would create opportunities for this sector of the economy. There would be periods of intense activity, in which they would work overtime through the night. But there were also periods of crisis, in which some of the workforce would be made redundant."* [12]

Textiles and socks factory in Sint-Niklaas

Mother Julia's job was as a supervisor responsible for checking stockings for faults

---

[11] Letter of Mother Julia, 18 May 1945.
[12] Mother Julia's Notes, 1945.

before they were shipped out for sale. In this way, she became acquainted with the situation of the women working in the mill: their joys and cares, their social attitudes, and how they worked, as well as their mentality and their spiritual disposition. She sought to develop their consciences. She encouraged those who worked diligently and honestly, but soon saw through those who were dishonest and did not do their duty, demanding that they should act justly and truthfully. She wanted to educate the workers to fulfil their duties faithfully, and to be honest and valued people. The managers of the mill held her in high regard, because she performed her duties with great care.

Mother Julia's health began to suffer as a result of the demands of work in the mill, and she discovered that she did not have as much time as she had hoped for the development of The Work. She tried to get the mill to give her a part-time job, but her efforts were to no avail, as she testified: *"I had hoped to gradually reduce my working hours, so that I would have more time to address the outstanding issues regarding The Work. But one can't expect my employer to understand this. I have tried in every way possible to find a solution."* [13]

As a result, Mother Julia left Verbreyt's mill at the end of August 1945 to look for another position. She was employed on a half-time basis as a seamstress by another firm in Sint-Niklaas. The owners of this company soon realised how gifted she was and were impressed by her charismatic personality. They detected in her an inspirational strength and asked her to assist in the running of their household. In spite of the reduction in her duties, on several occasions illness obliged her to take time off from work and to go away for periods of recuperation in the country.

In the meantime, Mother Julia's bond with those who were called to The Work grew stronger. She had also developed good relationships with some families, in whom she sensed a spiritual openness to the charism, and on occasion would stay with them for a few days. The mutual support that the consecrated women and the families could provide to each other was an important matter from the beginning. She was eager to share the joys and cares of families and form in them a Christian conscience.

The young women began to build up a library, even though they did not yet share a home together. Each of them was invited to make a contribution according to their means. To quote one of the circular letters: *"We already have a good collection of fine books, which can be used in our formation. We*

---

[13] Letter of Mother Julia, 11 August 1945.

would like all the books to be available to everyone. Therefore we are asking you to provide us with a list of all your books as soon as possible." [14] The library contained books in both Dutch and French. From the beginning, the variety of languages was seen as a source of enrichment.

The War had ended in Europe. From September 1944 the allies had gradually driven the German occupiers out of Belgium, and, on 8 May 1945, Germany's official surrender was signed in Berlin. The war had caused untold suffering. Approximately 55 million people lost their lives worldwide.[15] Many cities lay in ashes and ruins. Countless numbers of people suffered from hunger, poverty and destitution. Amongst the young in particular there was a spirit of great confusion.

After Germany's unconditional surrender the leaders of the allied powers – the American President Truman, the British Prime Minister Churchill, and the Soviet dictator Stalin – made radio broadcasts to their populations.[16] At Christmas, 1945, Pope Pius XII, too, addressed all of humanity in a radio talk. He stressed the fact that the world was still far from having established a real order of peace: *"Peace on earth? True peace? No: only the 'post-war period', to use a sad but very pregnant term! How long will it take to cure the material and moral disorder, to close up so many wounds! ... [A]nd today, when they must rebuild, men but faintly realize how much perspicacity and foresight, how much rectitude and good-will must go to the task of bringing the world back from physical and spiritual devastation and ruin to law, order, and peace."* [17]

Like many of the faithful throughout the world, those called to The Work strove with Mother Julia to work together for the building up of true peace. Through their lives, they sought to give an answer to the questions which they themselves asked: *"Are we ready to bear witness like Saint Paul to the Good News in the power of the spirit and with conviction? Do we want to be Sisters for these times in the spirit of Saint Paul? Are we messengers of happiness and peace?"* [18]

---

[14] Circular Letter in the spirit of Mother Julia, 9 January 1946.

[15] Cf. C. ESTEBAN and A. MUHLSTEIN (Eds.), *Grootboek van de Tweede Wereldoorlog*, first part: *Van München tot Pearl Harbor*, Amsterdam-Brussels: The Readers' Digest 1966, introduction to first part [9-11]; J. HART-MANN, *Das Geschichtsbuch. Von den Anfängen bis zur Gegenwart* (Fischer Taschenbücher 6314), Frankfurt: Fischer-Büchereit 1966, pp. 230 and 232-234.

[16] Cf. T. FLEMMING, A. STEINHAGE and P. STRUNK, *Chronik 1945. Tag für Tag in Wort und Bild*, Die Chronik-Bibliothek des 20. Jahrhunderts, Vol 45, ed. by B. Harenberg, Dortmund: Chronik Verlag ³1994, p. 92.

[17] Pius XII, *Negli ultimi sei anni* (Christmas Address to the College of Cardinals - 24 December 1945) in *Acta Apostolicae Sedis*, 38 (1946) 15-25, 15. Official English translation: 'English Text of Pope Pius' Address Outlining the Fundamentals for Effectuating Peace on Earth' in *New York Times*, 25 December 1945, p. 14.

[18] Circular Letter in the spirit of Mother Julia, 1 December 1945.

XVIII. Yearning for a common life

On 18 January 1945, the seventh anniversary of the founding of The Work, Mother Julia and the first group of vocations consulted with Fr Hillewaere about the ongoing development of The Work and the concrete steps they could take to live still more deeply in union with one another. At this meeting Mother Julia felt that the urge they all had to lead a common life had increased. She called this gathering a *"further milestone on the way to becoming a community"*, and stated: *"I am very content. I was able to detect a spontaneous and warm trust amongst them."* [1]

Mother Julia was moved by a deep-seated concern for souls in response to the needs of the times. She felt invited to do even more for the many young people, who had been marked by the effects of the war, and whose upbringing and education had been so frequently disrupted. She wrote to Fr Hillewaere: *"This concern drives me on to even greater perfection, to sacrifice, to abdication of self, to the surrender of my own person. This concern keeps me in living contact with the three Divine Persons. It allows me to experience Their unending help and presence through everything, and kindles in my heart a feeling of peace and joy, but also sometimes an unspeakable sadness."* [2]

A few months later the young Sisters gathered to make a retreat together for the first time. Fr Hillewaere had prepared the talks, but was unable to give them due to other pastoral duties. Another priest, a member of a religious order, took on responsibility for leading the retreat, using Fr Hillewaere's texts. In these days of reflection and prayer the Sisters were strengthened in the founding principles as followers of Christ in the spirit of The Work. The experience of the power of the sacraments and trust in the gifts of the Holy Spirit would empower them to grow in holiness, to regard the carrying out of God's will as the highest goal, and to be true apostles modelled on the first Christians. Mother Julia encouraged the Sisters to give their hearts completely to Christ and to overcome any human anxieties they might have. She wrote to one young woman: *"Look at Him and listen to Him in the stillness of your heart, in the stillness of His life amongst us in the*

---

[1] Letter of Mother Julia, 19 January 1945.
[2] *Ibid.*

Eucharist. He comes every day to share your life and to perfect it. Why then this fear, these disconcerting thoughts, which separate you from Him?" [3]

Because of her spirituality and her experience of life, Mother Julia was a life-giving presence and a model for the others. The following lines from a letter addressed to her show how grateful they all were: *"You are our model and understand how to give us courage time and again. You are 'the one who embodies the vocation' always and everywhere. We want to follow your way. Together we want to be The Work that is willed by God, to live according to it and to grow to maturity in it. Every day we want to be fervent apostles, who truly aspire to serve God and our neighbours. May faithful unity in Christ sustain us."* [4]

They felt inspired to act as daughters of the Church in the spirit of Saint Paul. One of them recalled: *"Right from the beginning Mother Julia taught us that the Apostle Paul was the patron of The Work, our leader and guide through his letters and teachings."* [5]

In preparation for another day of recollection the Sisters were encouraged to follow their calling with the following words in a circular letter: *"As individuals and as a group our watchword shall be: 'We bring life and renewal through the spirit of our vocation!' This means that we are now living our vocation, that we want to be The Work as it matures: in Christ Jesus, obedient to the will of the Father, in the power of the Holy Spirit, at Mary's side, in the service of the Church."* [6]

These and other gatherings strengthened the Sisters in their commitment to the Church and in their love of the charism. They used these days together to deepen their understanding of the fundamental truths of the Catholic Faith and to study topical issues, in order to have a better understanding of the signs of the times and to be better equipped for their apostolic service. They were also able to exchange details of what they experienced in their daily lives. Their different occupations and their apostolic work in Catholic Action on a parochial, regional and national level enriched their spiritual lives and broadened their appreciation of the needs of the post-war period. Catholic Action had assigned one of them to the running of a home for girls, who worked in the British Army barracks and were confronted with many personal and moral problems as a result.

In the summer of 1946, the brother of one of the Sisters found

---

[3] Letter of Mother Julia, 1945.
[4] Letter to Mother Julia, 22 May 1946.
[5] Recollections of Mother Julia, written down 1978.
[6] Circular Letter in the spirit of Mother Julia, 14 January 1946.

himself in difficulties. The young community helped him to look for accommodation for his family. After a short period of time they found a small house in Sint-Niklaas and made the first payment of rent. However, in the meantime, the father of the family had located a larger house. The community wondered what to do about the house they had found. Mother Julia discussed with Fr Hillewaere whether she and some of the Sisters should move into the house and begin to lead a life in common. A particular issue was how they would be able to afford to furnish the house and pay the monthly rent. Mother Julia placed her complete trust in God's Providence: *"He will take care of the material things Himself, if we follow His plan."* [7]

Mother Julia and Fr Hillewaere both considered that young people living together in a permanent community, and coming, as they did, from distinct social backgrounds, with different experiences from the war and the post-war period, was not simply a romantic idea. They knew that the newness and dynamism of the charism would place great demands on their communal life. In order to risk such a move, they needed a sign from heaven.

The young community prayed for enlightenment in this matter. Mother Julia was convinced that God would intercede, if they all fulfilled their duty towards the charism faithfully. She remarked to Fr Hillewaere: *"The present way of life of the Sisters has to lead to a life in community!"* [8] Although she knew that a common life suited to the charism had to evolve, she did not know how and when this would happen.

On 7 and 8 December 1946 Mother Julia met with the Sisters for two days of recollection. She reported later: *"Fr Hillewaere gave me the task of asking God for a clear sign concerning the growing community and whether it was His will that the members of The Work should start to live in common in this post-war period, and, if the answer was 'Yes', to reveal how this could be achieved concretely. This had become an ever more pressing question for Fr Hillewaere and the young women, who had discerned their vocation. A day of recollection was arranged for 7 December for all those who could make it. It was a day of prayer to prepare for the Solemnity of the Immaculate Conception. On 8 December, Fr Hillewaere invited the Sisters to come together to confront, as it were, this question for the first time. This took place at the presbytery in Menin, where he was parish priest."* [9]

---

[7] Letter of Mother Julia, 4 December 1946.
[8] *Ibid.*
[9] Letter of Mother Julia, 6 June 1975.

Presbytery of the parish of Saint Joseph in Menin

The young women had often received counsel and personal guidance from Fr Hillewaere in this house. They had been warmly welcomed on many occasions by Fr Hillewaere and his sister, who acted as his housekeeper. Unfortunately, as Mother Julia reported, the gathering on 8 December 1946 was not able to come up with a solution at first: *"The meeting was somewhat unsatisfactory. After they had all made their contribution, there still remained several unanswered questions concerning our life as a community. What direction were we to take? Ought we to live together or not?"* [10]

But, on the same evening, Providence sent a sign. This happened through a young man, the brother of one of the Sisters, whose parents Mother Julia had looked after for a long time: *"As I got out of the train in Sint-Niklaas, I met this young man, who informed me that his aunt had died. Her death had occurred unexpectedly exactly at the time of our meeting. From her inheritance, I received all the furniture from her house. As a result of this event, we understood that we were to live a common life as a family of God. As for material things, we received them all in abundance. The Lord Jesus and Mary, His Mother, were leading The Work onwards. It was a great sign from heaven for Fr Hillewaere, when he heard of God's wonderful intervention."* [11]

Some pieces of the furniture Mother Julia inherited

On that day God gave a clear sign. There could no longer be any doubt that a group of Sisters were to lead a common life in the small, empty house in Sint-Niklaas. They received so much furniture through this unexpected inheritance that they were even able to pass some of it on to others.

---

[10] Mother Julia's Notes, 24 August 1992.
[11] *Ibid.*

XIX. The community's first home

The young Sisters were very happy to be involved in establishing the community's new home with Mother Julia. They went about the necessary tasks with dedication, seeking to combine contemplation and readiness for action in their daily lives. Mother Julia wrote: *"We pray, we trust implicitly. In a spirit of tranquillity we build our little 'nest'. I want to pray with even greater confidence, to discuss everything, and to give myself to The Work of Jesus with my whole being and essence. In the meantime, we are continuing to make our little house clean and beautiful."* [1]

Although some of the Sisters were very busy in their jobs, and in spite of the geographical distance that separated them, they continued to find opportunities to spend time together for periods of deliberation and mutual support. At the beginning of 1947, the community gathered together in a retreat house for a few days of prayer and reflection, in order to prepare spiritually for the entry of the small group into the new home. After this gathering, Mother Julia wrote: *"I have the impression that it did them all good. I am very pleased. It gave us the opportunity to address and deliberate calmly on the outstanding questions concerning our little house. We were also able to consider the other questions concerning formation. It is a shame that the days went by so quickly. It was very good to be in an atmosphere of such peace with the Lord. The Blessed Sacrament was always exposed. The past year was a year of growth; it was blessed."* [2]

On the 9 April 1947, a few Sisters were finally able to begin to live the common life in the newly founded house in Sint-Niklaas. Julia was the 'mother' of the house and provided a sense of home and security. She guided the consciences of the Sisters who shared the life of the house with her. Some weeks after they had moved in, she wrote to one of the Sisters: *"Think about it – Jesus is the Unchanging One. Preserve in yourself an attitude of thankfulness. Show Him the trust of one who has been chosen, so that Truth may always accompany you and continually help you to gaze*

---

[1] Letter of Mother Julia, 17 December 1946.
[2] Letter of Mother Julia, 14 January 1947.

The community's first home in Sint-Niklaas

upon the Light. Be what you are – through God's grace!" [3]

Mother Julia made herself available with love and wisdom to those engaged in working in different locations, who would come 'home' on their days off, deepening the charism and enriching the family life. In this way there slowly developed a life lived by consecrated women, who strove to integrate a contemplative spirituality with an apostolic commitment, penetrating the world with the spirit of the charism.

One member of the first group of Sisters gave witness to the manner of formation: *"Where possible, Mother Julia would show the Sisters in simplicity and openness how they were to build their characters in virtue and self-denial, in order to attain balance in both the natural and supernatural spheres as religious. She could be so understanding and gentle, without being weak or falsely indulgent."* [4]

Mother Julia stressed that daily life with its many household tasks, often unnoticed by others, should be illuminated by the light of the charism. One Sister, who worked with her in the house, noted: "One day, as Mother Julia and I were painting the bedsteads in new colours, she suddenly asked me: 'Do you realise that what we are doing here and now is a contribution to a great work, for the salvation of the young, for those who are of good will?'" [5]

The young Sisters were to learn to think highly of the small things of everyday life and to fulfil their tasks in the spirit of their vocation and with apostolic endeavour.

Mother Julia placed great value on the performance of work with faith, devotion and love for the Church. A young Sister from that time remembered: *"One afternoon whilst I was sewing and Mother Julia was doing something else, she sang the 'Oremus' for the Holy Father and the Marian hymn, 'Sub tuum'. I became quite still, listening to these beautiful songs."* [6]

---

[3] Letter of Mother Julia, 20 April 1947.
[4] Recollections of Mother Julia, written down 24 October 2000.
[5] Recollections of Mother Julia, written down 1978.
[6] *Ibid.*

Mother Julia was aware from the outset that, in order to be genuine and healthy, the spiritual life had to remain bound to the practical tasks of everyday life. This was also true of financial matters. In a letter to Fr Hillewaere, she wrote: *"We have no more unpaid bills, even though lately we have had to purchase various things and to extend the loft. We lack nothing and there is even a little left over. It seems that Jesus is guiding The Work as it grows. Mary, our Mother, watches over The Work of Jesus, with all its weaknesses and limitations. We can do nothing, but sing with her the Magnificat in the depths of our souls: 'Magnificat anima mea Dominum'."* [7] In another letter she spoke of food, which was in such short supply in the post-war period: *"We are trying to maintain a healthy diet. I believe that the Sisters need that. Actually, we are not unduly concerned. We leave room for Divine Providence. But, the Lord certainly does not want us to be presumptuous in placing our trust in Him."* [8]

Along with her service in the house and in the work of formation, Mother Julia helped the young Sisters to gradually loosen their ties to their families. Before they moved into the little house the majority of them had lived with their parents or would frequently return home. During the war and in its immediate aftermath there had been no alternative. But now a way had opened, in which there was a possibility of following the evangelical counsels more closely. This involved disentangling and releasing themselves spiritually from their family ties. Mother Julia saw this clearly: *"To join the community means to leave one's parents' house and to give oneself to the Lord in The Work."* [9]

She helped the Sisters to achieve this letting-go resolutely, but at the same time with empathy and Christian prudence. This was not always easy. Mother Julia would try to help the parents to accept their daughters' vocations as a gift from God. Some parents showed their gratitude and goodwill by sending food to the young community. One family, which had produced several vocations, would regularly send milk, bread and vegetables. Others supported the community financially or by assisting in the house.

Their apostolic service also had to be infused with the fire of the charism. Mother Julia was anxious to lead the youthful enthusiasm of the Sisters to a maturity, in which their witness for Christ and the Church would be credible and attractive. She wrote: *"Apostolic service for others demands of us so much tact, so much sensitivity."* [10]

---

[7] Letter of Mother Julia, 12 October 1947.
[8] Letter of Mother Julia, 5 December 1947.
[9] Letter of Mother Julia, 1 October 1947.
[10] Letter of Mother Julia, 12 October 1947.

With an unswerving trust in God, she stood with those young people, who bore in their hearts a vocation to the consecrated life. With motherly love, she would give them advice and direction. Again and again, she indicated that they should build on the grace of their vocation and offer themselves without hesitation.

One aspirant, who got to know her in the little house in Sint-Niklaas in 1947, was deeply impressed by her personality. She testified: *"Above all, it was Mother Julia's charisma and winning nature that attracted me. She was so simple and honest. She was close to everyone. She was warm-hearted, relaxed. Nevertheless there was a distance there, which one cannot put into words. With Mother Julia there was true union as a family without any false familiarity. She was always a real lady, who inspired reverence by her very existence, without striving for it."* [11]

Through her being and actions Mother Julia had a great influence on the consciences of those around her. For some she was the instrument, through which they heard the silent call to closer discipleship and answered it in love. To one young girl, who had a vocation, she wrote: *"What grows in the silence of the soul must not be disturbed by the noise of words. It is so holy. Mary kept all those things that she had received from the Lord in her heart and pondered them. Silence is the environment, in which God can disclose Himself."* [12] In accepting young people into The Work she was not influenced by worldly criteria, such as status, qualifications, wealth, numbers and success. She always sought to know God's will. She wanted to lead all, who drew near to her on the way of conversion and faith, to a freely chosen 'Yes' to God's plan for them.

Mother Julia was careful not to make any rash decisions in accepting new members. She had a marked sense of truth and a very keen spirit of discernment. She once wrote about one young aspirant: *"I believe that we must not rush things with regards to her entry, but let things come to fruition. Above all, we too must grow with her, so that we become what God has called us to be."* [13]

The breadth of Mother Julia's spirit showed itself in her desire to live with the whole Church. She once told a priest: *"We unite our prayer during the International Week of Prayer for Christian Unity to the prayer of all the faithful children of the Church, that more and more we may become one – to the glory and honour of God, for the good and unity of the Church."* [14] She

---

[11] Recollections of Mother Julia, written down 24 October 2000.
[12] Letter of Mother Julia, 28 February 1947.
[13] Letter of Mother Julia, 12 May 1947.
[14] Letter of Mother Julia, 17 January 1947.

was very interested in the latest developments in Church and society, and possessed a finely tuned sense for the new trends, which were making their mark on the times. She had a thoroughly contemplative and apostolic heart. In response to a woman who was active in the Young Catholic Workers, who questioned how a new development in the movement could be possible, she wrote: *"We must awaken a new spirit of faith based on the model of the first Christians. An intense spiritual life is necessary for a fruitful apostolate in the world. At the same time we must take account of external circumstances and the possibilities they contain."* [15]

At that time, several Sisters were working in the large restaurant of the Young Catholic Workers' Centre in Brussels.[16] One of them was responsible for the waitresses. One day she sought advice from Mother Julia, as these young women came from very different backgrounds. Mother Julia gave her clear guidelines on how she, as a consecrated woman, was to carry out her apostolic service: *"With reference to your being in the Centre you must keep two things in view: your formation as a person and your work. In this you will find guidelines for your conduct and your apostolate – how to behave as one of those called to The Work in your dealings with the girls working as waitresses. I stress emphatically 'as one called', because our being called has its own spirit and its own method for the apostolate. Our apostolate flows from contemplation. Your greatest influence on the others lies in your performing your duties as a waitress just like them. This will help you to fulfil your educative role amongst the others through your conduct."* [17]

Mother Julia worked tirelessly to bring the Sisters together as a family of God. She constantly emphasised the power that came from the gift of the 'Holy Covenant': *"Bound in unity with Christ, we offer ourselves up for His intentions and are secure in the great grace of the 'Holy Covenant'."*[18] Permeated with this light, she was able to anticipate the future and to develop a form of common life that did not exist in the Church at that time.

On 2 February 1947, the apostolic constitution, '*Provida Mater*', had appeared, in which Pope Pius XII gave Secular Institutes official canonical recognition. As the Church had now recognised the consecrated life lived in the world, Mother Julia and Fr Hillewaere felt strengthened in their search for a canonical structure for the charism. At the same time they were aware, and were confirmed in this view as the development of the charism took

---

[15] Letter of Mother Julia, 12 November 1947.
[16] Cf. L. ALAERTS, *Door eigen werk sterk*, pp. 179 and 202.
[17] Letter of Mother Julia, 6 November 1947.
[18] Letter of Mother Julia, 9 July 1947.

its course, that while certain elements of the charism bore similarities to Secular Institutes, others were quite different and were not compatible with their objectives. They continued to accompany the young community in faith and with patience, trusting that in His own time the Lord would send ecclesiastical recognition in a form applicable to the charism.

It became increasingly clear to them that those called to The Work were not to lead a common life in the traditional sense, nor to follow an individual apostolate in the manner of Secular Institutes. Rather their mission was to live as a family of God in the spirit of Saint Paul and the early Church. They had a high regard for the way of life of the traditional religious orders and understood their significance for the Church, but were conscious nevertheless of the need for The Work to develop in a different direction. The community life in this spiritual family was to be distinctive on account of its clear rejection of the spirit of the world, and not because it was enclosed or because of an external separation from the world. Mother Julia would often make the point that the Sisters were to use their talents, gifts and graces in the service of the Church, whilst at the same time developing a truly common life.

It was understandable that this new form of common life would raise questions and lead to misconceptions in some circles, because it departed from the forms of the consecrated life that were recognised at that time. But Mother Julia was convinced that, in respect of the form of common life they were to pursue, she was obliged to follow the route she had recognised in conscience as intended by God. In later years, she wrote: *"Those called should find inspiration in the first Christian communities, and in faith, virtue and devotion cultivate the life of a true family of God through their shared thinking, experience and action in the grace of unity."* [19]

In her search and struggles, Mother Julia always possessed an inner awareness of the greatness of the charism and its mission for the universal Church, although only the very beginnings were externally visible. *"It seems to me"*, she wrote, *"that The Work must grow into a work that builds up the Church. I see how the vocation responds to and meets the needs of the Church. At the same time, I can see how the life of the Church flows into the vocation."* [20]

---

[19] Mother Julia's Notes, 18 January 1970.
[20] Letter of Mother Julia, 4 December 1946.

XX. Life and formation in the city

The house in Sint-Niklaas soon became too small for the growing community, and the question arose as to whether the Sisters should not move to Brussels. For some time, Mother Julia had wished to be able to provide better leadership to the Sisters working in Brussels. So, a few of the Sisters were charged with making enquiries about this possibility, and soon found a suitable house. They were able to raise the large deposit through their own means and with the assistance of benefactors, and within a short period of time the tenancy agreement was signed.

The community left Sint-Niklaas on 7 January 1948, and moved into its new home in Brussels. The move changed the situation significantly. Now, the charism had to be lived in a city, where there were many possibilities, but also new challenges. Mother Julia was aware of the great responsibility on her and the young Sisters to develop their vocation to the consecrated life in this environment.

Acquiring a larger house was a blessing for their common life. In Sint-Niklaas only a few of the Sisters could live permanently with Mother Julia. Now the number living in common increased, as those who had been in Brussels for some time joined the community. Other Sisters who were employed and involved in apostolic work in Flanders would come regularly to Brussels to gain new strength at the source of the charism. Mother

First house in Brussels-
St Gilles

Julia supported and motivated them all in their life of consecration.

As the Sisters grew together in their common life, they were filled with joy and confidence. At the same time they became increasingly aware of the demands that such a life placed on them. Mother Julia called on them to fight the good fight of faith, according to the model of Saint Paul, and to see the challenges of everyday life as opportunities for personal and communal growth as followers of Christ. She endeavoured to make a real home for them all and to lead them forward. One Sister remembered: *"When we lived in Ducpétiaux Avenue in Brussels, Mother Julia was in charge of the household. She cooked and cleaned. What was especially striking about her was the love with which she performed all her tasks. She was always trying something new in the kitchen and in her welcome to the Sisters, providing them with a true home and real community, so that we were always glad to return."* [1]

In her role as mother of the house she was concerned that any resources they possessed should be used responsibly. At the same time there burned in her heart an unswerving trust in God's Providence. Once, at the end of a month, the community ran out of food, a common experience amongst many families after the Second World War. So they opened the Bible at random and read the following passage from the Sermon on the Mount: *"Do not be anxious about your life, what you shall eat .... Look at the birds of the air: they neither sow nor reap nor gather into barns, and yet your heavenly Father feeds them.... But seek first his kingdom and his righteousness, and all these things shall be yours as well"* (Mt 6:25-33). One of the Sisters recorded: *"That same evening a Sister returned from a visit to her family with a large trunk, full of all kinds of foodstuffs."* [2]

Tabernacle in the parish church of Saint Alena in Brussels

The warm and sacred atmosphere created by Julia's motherly nature, benefited the young Sisters. They felt accepted and loved: *"I think I may say"*, wrote Mother Julia, *"that I love them just as they are before Jesus."* [3] It was in the heart of her Divine Bridegroom, especially through the Mass, silent prayer and meditation on the Gospels, that she found the strength to give this love to others.

Mother Julia performed her household duties happily and loved being together with the Sisters. At the same time she felt herself drawn spiritually to the tabernacle in the parish church. (There was at that time no chapel in

---

[1] Recollections of Mother Julia, written down 8 November 2000.
[2] Recollections of Mother Julia, written down 1978.
[3] Letter of Mother Julia, 5 June 1948.

their house.) Whilst praying in adoration, she often felt an inner anguish, because in the busy city so few people visited the Blessed Sacrament. She declared once: *"I would dearly love to be there all the time, making expiation. I am striving more and more to be the living tabernacle of Jesus in the midst of the demands of everyday life."* [4]

Mother Julia was particularly concerned to keep alive amongst all the Sisters their joy in the vocation of The Work. On the feast of the Sacred Heart, 1948, she called for special thanks for God's good deeds, and wrote about it later: *"After breakfast we devoutly sang the 'Te Deum' together in thankfulness for everything that the Lord has given us, so that we might share his thirst for souls."* [5]

In reading and meditating on the Gospels, she was struck by how the Lord taught his followers and by how glorious it is to lead a life of close discipleship. She informed Fr Hillewaere: *"I love reading the passages in the Gospels, in which Jesus instructs His Apostles. How powerfully He teaches and acts! Oh, Father, we have so much to learn from Him. Yesterday was the feast of the Sacred Heart. The memory of it overwhelms my soul. My whole being rejoices in wonder at being allowed to give myself to Him as His bride."* [6]

Apart from caring for the house and creating a spiritual atmosphere in the community, Mother Julia saw the formation of the Sisters as her most important task. Each of them required being led personally and reverently in accordance with God's plan for them, so that their talents, gifts and graces could be developed in faithfulness to the charism.

Although Mother Julia had received no formal education beyond elementary school, she was a teacher in heart and soul, never forgetting that the true teacher is Jesus Christ Himself. After a day of recollection, she wrote to Fr Hillewaere: *"Sunday was a retreat day. There was an atmosphere like Pentecost, which has continued. Jesus shares freely the graces of the 'Holy Covenant' amongst His little flock. If you could witness it, your soul would leap for joy and give thanks! Jesus let me understand that His little flock brings Him much joy. He wants to instruct them in a particular way, so that they can withstand the spirit of the times."* [7]

Fr Hillewaere would have liked to go to Brussels more often to be with the community and to give them talks on theological and spiritual themes. But, the pressing obligations of his pastoral work in the large parishes of

[4] Letter of Mother Julia, 7 July 1948.
[5] Letter of Mother Julia, 5 June 1948.
[6] *Ibid.*
[7] Letter of Mother Julia, 7 October 1948.

Menin and later in Zwevegem plus the geographical distance meant he could only make occasional visits. This was a great sacrifice both for him and for the community. However, he was thankful that the Passionists, who had a monastery in Wezembeek, near Brussels, were committed to assisting Mother Julia and the community with their priestly service. Fr Herman and two of his confreres showed a particular openness to the vocation of The Work. And so a mutually fruitful co-operation developed between the two communities.

From the beginning Mother Julia tried to provide the Sisters with a rounded formation. Every area of human life had to be related to what was specific to The Work. She underlined the fact that the Sisters had not joined an apostolic group or movement, but a spiritual family, to which God had given its own charism and its own spirit. On one occasion she expressed it this way: *"The young people who are called must not receive a formation as if they belonged to a movement and remained in the world or could choose another form of life. Trusting in the grace of their vocation, they must be formed in a way that conforms entirely to the life and mission of The Work."* [8]

Mother Julia argued that what mattered most in the consecrated life was loving obedience to the will of God: *"Whoever enters must be ready for unconditional commitment. I ask that in everything the will of God be accomplished and that God is loved more and more!"* [9] In The Work, this total dedication took on the form of a 'Holy Covenant' with the Heart of Jesus. Thus, Mother Julia called ceaselessly for love for the Heart of Jesus and steadfast trust in the grace of the 'Holy Covenant'.

She helped the Sisters to learn to bear responsibility. She knew how important the virtue of moderation was: conscientious commitment, dynamic readiness for service and selfless dedication had to be combined with Christian sagacity and steadiness – and this was not easy for young people. Mother Julia tried to lead the first generation to this awareness by her example: *"It seems to me that the young people around me have yet to learn what it means and demands to take on responsibility. I am endeavouring to help them understand by acting as their example, in so far as this is possible."* [10] Alongside responsibility for personal discipleship of Christ and apostolic activity and service in the world, the Sisters were to be brought to

---

[8] Letter of Mother Julia, 9 February 1947.
[9] Letter of Mother Julia, 17 March 1948.
[10] Letter of Mother Julia, 29 January 1948.

understand the need to take on responsibility for their spiritual family: *"The will of God includes for us, who regard ourselves as having a vocation, readiness for service in The Work of Jesus. We have experienced this daily in so far as we have given ourselves and responded positively to the will of God. Our vocation encompasses the whole of life. The apostolate of the first group of vocations lies in building up The Work in its all-encompassing sense."* [11]

Mother Julia strove to help the Sisters develop into mature women. In the spirit of unity and of mutual love, she sought to show them *"the way to a self-knowledge supported by grace and humility"* and to loving devotion to the Heart of Jesus. *"I attribute so much value to this grace"*, she informed Fr Hillewaere, *"that words actually fail me. I call it a special grace, because it encompasses to such a high degree the gift of faith in love, which leads us on the way of the cross to pure and complete devotion to the bridegroom. I think I can say that, since this insight was given to me, I have refused Jesus nothing, in order to merit this special grace for the Sisters."* [12]

She recognised early on the dangers of the increasing influence of individualism for the consecrated life. She helped the Sisters to accept themselves entirely and to develop everything pure and good that God had placed in them. At the same time, she warned them against striving after honour and a career, and often pointed out that the orientation to a communal way of thinking was of fundamental significance. Accordingly, she wrote to one Sister, who had many gifts, but was still too attached to her own desires and ideas: *"Dear Sister, you have not joined a work that is just there for the sake of your individual vocation. The goal of The Work is to be a spiritual family and to nurture a common life that embraces all of life. Therefore, we are not at liberty to give free rein to our personal thoughts and feelings. Because the Lord Himself demands it, we are obliged to follow the road that He has laid out for everyone whom He calls to this Work."* [13]

Above all else, Mother Julia wanted to form and anchor the consciences of the Sisters in the truth and love of Christ. She once wrote: *"It seems to me that for everyone the demand to make further progress, in an honest and spontaneous striving after truth, is increasing. May we not then expect with even greater trust that Jesus who says of Himself: 'I am the Truth', will become more and more our Way and our Life?"* [14] With a joyful and thankful heart, she declared: *"A spirit of sisterly love, simplicity and truth prevails. There is*

---

[11] Letter of Mother Julia, 17 March 1948.
[12] Letter of Mother Julia, 18 October 1948.
[13] Letter of Mother Julia, 9 May 1948.
[14] Letter of Mother Julia, 22 April 1948.

complete conformity with the foundational principles of the vocation." [15]

Mother Julia shed the light of the charism on every situation: in meetings and retreats, in her talk at meal times, in the preparation for the liturgy, in introducing others to specific tasks, in walks and on the way to the Church, in visits and unexpected encounters, in communal gatherings, in personal contacts and in responding to questions addressed to her.

In addition to the formation in daily life, she regarded the reading of appropriate spiritual literature as very important. She recognised how important for a truly contemplative life is a love that desires to serve. At the same time, she understood the significance of the unadulterated doctrine of the faith for healthy development in the spiritual life. In order to find good books for the community, she would consult with Fr Hillewaere, who had acquired a wide-ranging knowledge of theological and spiritual issues. When she recommended the reading of particular works to the Sisters, she would often explain how they should be understood in the present context and in the spirit of their vocation.

Once, as one of the Sisters was undergoing an inner struggle, Mother Julia felt that she needed some help: *"I advised her to use a book for meditation, to put in place a daily routine, and to fulfil her daily duties faithfully and steadfastly, to examine her conscience at night, to think of the Lord often during the day and to maintain union with Him."* [16] Mother Julia was aware of the danger of seeking pleasure even in spiritual things. Therefore, she wanted books to be read in a spirit of discernment and with an inner discipline, and the knowledge acquired to be translated into acts of faith. She was in complete agreement with Fr Hillewaere about this: *"The great danger is that one forgets what is important: the Holy Spirit. Then one also forgets to prepare souls to be open to the workings of the Holy Spirit, through renunciation, humility and trust, through a sincere disposition, through a life of prayer. One 'knows' a lot, but does not 'do' a lot."* [17]

Sometimes Mother Julia warned of an idle curiosity in reading. Even when she was young, she had felt that she must not simply read whatever she liked. A few years before her death she told one of the Sisters how the Lord had guided her in this matter and had thus spared her many difficulties: *"The vocation was able to develop by quite natural and supernatural means according to God's plan. I did not compare myself with others and I had no*

---

[15] Letter of Mother Julia, 8 February 1948.
[16] Letter of Mother Julia, 20 July 1948.
[17] Letter of Mother Julia, 1 December 1948.

yearning for books on mysticism. I was compelled to offer myself as a sacrifice. I received the vocation; I did not discover or work it out myself. We must respond to the graces we are given and not call them into question." [18]

Although Mother Julia was primarily concerned with the care of her own community, she never forgot those around her. She had a big, loving, Catholic heart. She once noticed that a priest was showing signs of overwork and feeling a little depressed. With sisterly concern and a certain boldness, she approached him: *"You must find time to rest. I am praying for you more than ever. I can understand that your responsibilities are sometimes burdensome to you. But I do not see why a sense of responsibility should make us anxious, it should rather lead to greater faith, to greater trust, to a deeper understanding of our powerlessness and dependence on the Lord."* [19]

Mother Julia felt compelled to help those people experiencing hardship, whom Providence placed in her path. One day when she was shopping in the town, she saw a man who had collapsed in the street, while out with his daughter. She quickly assessed the situation, provided first aid and arranged for the man to be taken to hospital. The casualty was Jewish, and his family had suffered greatly during the war. Several members of his family had died in concentration camps. Only the girl and her father had survived and they now lived in the slum area of Brussels. The father survived the heart attack and, after a while, was able to leave the clinic. Mother Julia visited him several times, and remained friends with him and his daughter for many years.

On another occasion she visited two mines in the industrial part of Liège. She was upset that there were so few workers in the vineyard of the Lord willing to care for these people. The situation of an Orthodox priest, who worked in the mines, but also had to care for the many migrant workers, also touched her heart. She understood his difficulties and gave him encouragement.

She was particularly concerned with young people. *"One of the most important duties of our vocation"*, she wrote, *"is spiritual motherhood of the parentless youth of our times."* [20] In the city, she saw that many young people were growing up almost without an upbringing, 'parentless'. Often they did have parents, who looked after their everyday needs, but did not fully recognise the requirement to educate them. The spirit of materialism,

[18] Conversation with Mother Julia, February 1994.
[19] Letter of Mother Julia, 17 March 1948.
[20] Letter of Mother Julia, 10 March 1948.

permissiveness and of the new heathenism began to spread more widely. Mother Julia was convinced that parents had to be helped with love and respect and that many young people needed to be given real direction.

She had learnt her love and zeal for souls from Saint Paul, and wanted to lead the Sisters to this same thirst for souls. She wrote to Fr Hillewaere, *"God is good. Let us surrender ourselves to Him in these distressing times. Let us offer him an unconditional and unlimited surrender without counting the cost! Then we will hear Him, see Him, experience Him in the life, which arises and unfolds around us. Father, I long to share this with the Sisters, so that they may be seized by a love and thirst to give themselves, to forget themselves, in order to be all things to all men."* [21]

---

[21] Letter of Mother Julia, 16 June 1948.

XXI. In the service of families

Before the First World War there had been several initiatives to help women and mothers in their many tasks. After the horror of this war many parishes put in place organisations, offering valuable services to mothers. The goal of these groups was to build up, strengthen and nurture Christian family life. The 'Women's Association of the Christian Worker Movement' was formed in Flanders in 1932 out of such previously existing organisations, and expanded rapidly.[1]

The Second World War caused new hardship and misery to many families. Consequently, during the years following the war, the 'Women's Association of the Christian Worker Movement', which operated within Catholic Action, and other organisations developed the idea of supporting young families, especially if the mother was ill or pregnant. As a consequence, a need was identified for well-trained assistants, who were capable of helping mothers, and, if necessary, of taking over their responsibilities for a time. Although the different groups had the same goal, they followed their own direction and their own way of working. In 1944, the 'People's Movement for the Family' was founded in Wallonia, emerging from the Young Catholic Workers, and developed into an influential mature movement for adults. However, they soon ended their involvement in Catholic Action, in order to be able to fulfil their mission in the service of the family without political and religious restrictions.[2]

In 1948 Mother Julia and the young community came into contact with the leadership of the French-speaking section of the 'Women's Association of the Christian Worker Movement'. This group had begun in Brussels with the setting-up of a family assistance service and was able to attract a few women to act as family helpers. However, their numbers remained too few, and it proved difficult to find more women willing to take on this work.

---

[1] Cf. L. ALAERTS, *Door eigen werk sterk*, p. 204.
[2] Cf. *ibid.*, pp. 396-397; A. OSAER, 'De christelijke arbeidersvrouwenbeweging' in E. GERARD (Ed.), *De christelijke arbeidersbeweging in België* (Kadoc-Studies 11), Leuven: Universitaire Pers 1991, pp. 372-374 and 382-383.

A few months previously, it had become clear during conversations between Fr Hillewaere and the national leadership of the female branch of the Young Catholic Workers that, given the fundamental differences in approach, the continued involvement of The Work was becoming untenable, and that a separation was inevitable. In this situation Mother Julia and the Sisters involved in working with families saw an opportunity to work with a different grouping within Catholic Action for the renewal of the Church and society. The leadership of the 'Women's Association of the Christian Worker Movement' were happy and thankful for their participation. Mother Julia saw a way of further developing the charism in this activity, which

Sisters of The Work in the service of families

also had a missionary character: *"It seems at this moment in time that there has opened up a valuable area of work and apostolate in the service of the family."* [3]

From the outset they had had at heart a concern for a joyful and faithful family spirit – in married couples and families, as well as in their own community and in the Church. In a letter to Fr Hillewaere, Mother Julia expressed her joy that one of the Sisters was especially suited for this task: *"I rejoice with our Sister. I hope that she will get the opportunity for personal development. In silence we watch for what this development will bring. The main thing it seems to me now is that our Sisters should give themselves generously and be of service to others without hesitation at every opportunity. Our Lord, whose generosity is unsurpassed, will certainly make up for what we lack. In view of the hardships and the gravity of the current situation, we are compelled to serve people, to bear witness to the Lord, to pass on the merciful love that He has given us and to draw it down on others through our faithfulness. It is so, so urgent!"* [4]

The leaders of the family service quickly recognised that this Sister of The Work had a talent for organisation and fulfilled her responsibilities diligently. As a result she was soon entrusted with more important tasks

---

[3] Letter of Mother Julia, 27 October 1948.
[4] Letter of Mother Julia, 2 August 1948.

and later with leadership responsibilities. In the following months, as the requests for help increased, more Sisters began to take on this work. They attended courses in order to gain the necessary qualifications, the examinations for which took place before a State commission.

Mother Julia and the Sisters saw the family assistance service in Brussels as providing them with the possibility of leavening society with a Christian spirit and of developing further their mission of apostolic service in faithfulness to the charism. Their concern was to strengthen and to encourage good families in the faith. They also supported families that found themselves in material, moral or religious difficulties, teaching them human and Christian principles. This service opened up ways for the community to work in collaboration with the clergy and with people in various ecclesiastical positions, to bear witness to the charism, and to make explicit how their vocation was orientated towards the Church.

In the letters that Mother Julia wrote at the time, she spoke constantly about the situations, in which the community could render assistance. She saw how spiritual destitution often led to social misery and damaged the development of the young. She wanted to support them with the grace of the charism: *"I believe that these and other insights are pushing me to promote help to the family in this way. I am continually conferring with the Lord about the destitute condition of souls and the concerns of The Work, which are those of the Church. And it seems to me that the Lord with His gaze almost always lets me understand His insights."* [5]

The principle of leading people through personal contact was particularly important to her. The service to families provided many natural opportunities for being involved with others and witnessing to the power of the Gospel. She told of one woman, who had been separated from her husband for some time: *"It seems that she has written a letter to her husband for the first time, admitting the blame on her side and asking for forgiveness. May the Lord help her with His all-conquering grace and be merciful to her!"* [6]

She watched the many positive developments with joy and humility: *"I think that we have to work further in this direction without haste. The matter is clear and simple. I do not expect that no difficulties will present themselves or that no failures can occur. Yesterday afternoon our Sister was called to a meeting with the priest in charge. He has accepted all our proposals*

---

[5] Letter of Mother Julia, 21 February 1949.
[6] Letter of Mother Julia, 23 May 1950.

and given us complete freedom to develop initiatives and ideas about how to work. The leadership have made clear their high regard for our young group in its service to families. It appears that people are extremely content. What strikes them most is the spirit of fellowship." [7]

The woman responsible for the day-to-day running of the family service was very pleased at the trouble-free way in which the young Sisters had integrated themselves into their work. She exclaimed: *"I don't understand it. These young women live in such unity. How the good God blesses us!"* [8] Mother Julia was thankful that the spirit of the charism was bearing fruit in the family service, but, unimpressed by human praise, appended the following remark in a letter: *"Now, will this admiration last? Let's hope so!"* [9]

Mother Julia was convinced that the community had to become increasingly a spiritual family in the service of the Church, and addressed the Sisters with words filled with a spiritual fire: *"Create an atmosphere, in which deep understanding, holy reverence and heroic virtue increase and lead us to that perfection, which is worthy of our vocation. In Christ I can as it were see the things and ideas of this world as well as the current state of affairs with its dangers for the Church and for souls. In the light of these experiences there is a particular grace, through which the Lord wishes to unite Himself with us: The Work. It seems to me that He wants to work powerfully towards the building-up of The Work from within and that we must continue to work in this direction. What is external must be born out of this inner growth. Everything external must get its form and vigour from within. It is the Lord's will. It is as if He gives us to understand that He Himself will stand surety for everything that is necessary for life. He Himself wishes to be the one in charge. He would like to strengthen His dominion over those who are called, in a way that is so powerful and complete that by the realisation of His plans they become His compliant instruments and His true witnesses."* [10]

Requests for assistance in the work with families continued to grow. They came not only from the leadership of the 'Women's Association of the Christian Worker Movement', but also from the 'People's Movement for the Family', in which Sisters from The Work were also involved. Several parishes in Brussels and the neighbouring area, as well as private individuals, with whom they were developing increasingly close contacts,

---

[7] Letter of Mother Julia, 8 February 1949.
[8] *Ibid.*
[9] *Ibid.*
[10] Letter of Mother Julia, 26 October 1944 and 3 February 1949.

also requested help. Mother Julia saw that the many demands and requests were gradually leading to a situation in which the Sisters were taking on too much. As a consequence, the community reached the decision to engage other young women as helpers in the service alongside the Sisters.

The Sisters wanted to provide those women interested in the work with families a real home in their own centre and to give them a professional, personal and religious education. Mother Julia called on the consecrated Sisters to provide a good example by their joy in the faith and in their determination to follow Christ. She was also concerned to prepare the assistants for married and family life or for closer discipleship.

It was at this time that the community developed the idea of founding their own association for the formation of these young women. Mother Julia wrote in a letter: *"We anticipate that the lawyer will soon start work on the draft for a state recognised, non-profit making association. We are thinking of calling it 'St Paul's House'. The character of the project must not be too cloistered."* [11] On 19 March 1949, 'St Paul's House' received state recognition.[12] With the creation of this association, they had laid the legal foundations for the training of family assistants, who did not belong to the community.

The Sisters prepared a brochure for the opening, in which the aims of the association were explained and which quoted the hymn concerning love in Paul's *First Letter to the Corinthians*. The name, 'St Paul's House', was intended to express what it was that inspired the community: Paul was their patron and their great role model. The Sisters wanted to follow His teaching, his way of life, his missionary activity for the kingdom of God. Their aim was to offer a home to many, from which they could draw strength and where they could experience a true, Christian love of neighbour.

With the introduction into the family service of the assistants involved in 'St Paul's House', it soon became clear that the house of The Work was too small, and that further accommodation would have to be rented. At the same time Mother Julia and the community thought of using the house just for those involved in the family service, and of acquiring a separate house for the Sisters not officially involved, so that they could develop new possibilities outside of the family service. *"I would like the Sisters to become progressively capable of responding humbly and proficiently to these and to other initiatives, which come their way in the future."* [13]

---

[11] Letter of Mother Julia, 7 October 1948.
[12] Cf. *Belgisch Staatsblad/Moniteur belge* 19 March 1949, record No 706.
[13] Letter of Mother Julia, 21 February 1949.

The house in Wezembeek-Oppem

On 3 August 1949, the Sisters, who were not engaged in working with families, moved to Wezembeek, a suburb of Brussels, where a benefactor had helped them purchase a house. This house brought new opportunities. Whilst the Sisters lived in the same house as the family assistants, it was difficult to develop their consecrated vocation and common life further, since they always had to take account of the assistants. Now the community – including those involved in apostolic work in Flanders – would gather with joy and thankfulness for days of recollection in Wezembeek. Mother Julia wrote to Fr Hillewaere: *"The move is complete and a second house has been entrusted to our care. The Lord appears to direct everything Himself. It is calm and tranquil here. On Sunday we had the first retreat day for the Sisters. We took as the subject of our reflection the 'little Rule', the presentations from the spiritual exercises of 1945 and a text from Saint Paul. We chose these texts with a view to living our Rule more intensely. We have more possibilities as a result of the space and must not adapt it for the family assistants."* [14]

Whilst some of the Sisters settled into the new house in Wezembeek and others continued to work for the family service, tensions arose between the 'Women's Association of the Christian Worker Movement' and the 'People's Movement for the Family'.

Mother Julia saw the problems that collaboration with these two organisations brought with it as a challenge, to persevere in faith and to co-operate patiently with God's plan. She wanted to avoid ill-considered and hasty decisions. She and the Sisters worked to achieve a new understanding between the two organisations: *"It is clear to us – and the Sisters are agreed – that we must do whatever is possible to prevent a split."* [15] Because of the efforts on all sides it was possible to overcome the difficulties for a period. At the same time, increasing numbers of private individuals, who had no contact with the official organisations supporting the family, turned to the community.

---

[14] Letter of Mother Julia, 24 August 1949.
[15] Letter of Mother Julia, 25 July 1949.

The work with families was very demanding, but also very rewarding. Mother Julia wrote in a letter: *"It seems that the leaders of the family service have realised that the Sisters are really capable, both on a professional level and in their apostolic commitment. It has been decided that each of them is to be responsible for the family service in two or three parishes."* [16]

It was not only within the family service that the Sisters were respected and esteemed. For example, a well-known musician organised a charitable concert for the community as a thank you for the help they had given him. His wife had died giving birth to their sixth child, and one of the Sisters had supported the family for some months during this difficult time. The media also became interested, and there were some positive reports on the radio. Various parishes were glad for the service. Mother Julia wrote: *"We are very pleased that the involvement of The Work in the family service is recognised and accepted by the clergy. Several of them thought that there had to be a distinctive charism behind this work. Yesterday evening a parish priest asked for a short report that he could publish in his parish newsletter. He thought that such a community ought to be made known and supported."* [17]

This parish priest, and other people too, felt that the young women were filled with a unique spirit. Mother Julia attached great importance to the fact that the Sisters had gained the trust of people by their faithful service and their professional commitment in whatever they did, and that they brought them closer to Christ and the Church. Because their charism did not require them to wear a particular religious habit, they could operate more effectively as yeast in those sections of society that were becoming increasingly distanced from Christian principles. The first Christians were their models in this.

Mother Julia encouraged the Sisters to believe in God's power and love: *"Let us have confidence! What seemed to be impossible yesterday can with God's grace become possible tomorrow. Let us work together for this one objective without wasting strength or time: the glorification of God in the kingdom of souls!"* [18]

One of the Sisters, who found herself engaged in difficult work, received encouragement from Mother Julia with the following words: *"It is the easiest and also the one right thing: Wherever the Lord has allotted us our place, we should live wholeheartedly and accept reality, just as it is. If, then,*

---

[16] Letter of Mother Julia, 4 August 1949.
[17] Letter of Mother Julia, 23 June 1949.
[18] Letter of Mother Julia, 2 April 1948.

we find ourselves in a situation that overwhelms us, we will have the goodwill to learn gladly and not flinch at the difficulties or the burden. For we know that this makes us able to serve better. O simplicity, mirror and image of the divine being! May we all be filled with it abundantly!" [19]

After a period of co-operation, serious difficulties arose once more between the two organisations involved in the family service. After negotiations between the leadership of Catholic Action in Wallonia and Cardinal Van Roey, the Archbishop of Mechelen (1926-1961), the two organisations were merged and the 'People's Movement for the Family' disbanded.[20] This led to new problems and unrest amongst the assistants and families that they served. Mother Julia wrote: *"I do not see what else we can do in this situation except pray, make sacrifices and bring our concerns to the Lord, so that He will guide and channel everything according to His judgement and pleasure. Until matters become clear, we will strive with complete commitment for the total fulfilment of our duty in every moment. I have great trust. I must confess that such storms sometimes inflict all kinds of suffering on me, but sometimes they fill me with great peace and a profound joy. It seems to me that the Lord has the situation in hand, and that through it He wishes to sanctify and purify our vocation for His glorification."* [21]

Mother Julia rejoiced at the nobility and beauty revealed in the Sisters' apostolic commitment. But with her balanced sense of judgement, she also recognised their weaknesses and limits. How were the Sisters to overcome this in the light of the charism? *"We too have weaknesses"*, Mother Julia asserted in relation to the collaboration with the family service of Catholic Action, *"but we must pre-empt our sinful inclinations through unity and mutual support. We must fight the good fight together in the light of our vocation. We must complement each other in love."* [22]

Since the time that Mother Julia had entered into the 'Holy Covenant', and, even more, since The Work had come into being with the foundation of the community in 1938, she had felt called to offer up her life out of love for the Church for the good of her spiritual family. Now she felt even more clearly the Lord's desire to lead the Sisters to a higher level in their personal growth and apostolic activity: *"I believe that the Lord is preparing a new direction. I praise Him and thank Him for everything."* [23]

---

[19] Letter of Mother Julia, 19 August 1949.
[20] Cf. L. ALAERTS, *Door eigen werk sterk*, p. 397.
[21] Letter of Mother Julia, 30 November 1949.
[22] Conversation with Mother Julia, 21 February 1994.
[23] Letter of Mother Julia, 31 January 1950.

This new direction revealed itself in August 1948 in a concrete development involving Fr Hillewaere. After a meeting with Canon Cardijn at which they discussed the future of The Work, he withdrew completely from his involvement with the Young Catholic Workers. Canon Cardijn's movement had spread across Europe and to other continents in the years after the Second World War. In the words of Lee Alaerts, this brought *"new influences, interpretations and ways of thinking. The post-war generation was characterised by a greater diversity."* [24] There were clear differences of emphasis in the movement's objectives. The approach to their work was adapted to society's different needs and its increasing prosperity. The social element was ranked above the religious, and growing individualism pushed the experience of community into the background. A kind of humanism gained a foothold, *"a life focusing on human values slowly became an end in itself".* [25]

Fr Hillewaere recognised that in conscience he had to go in a different direction. Along with his duties as a parish priest, he now wanted to promote even more explicitly the internal and external growth of The Work and to use his priestly authority to assist the community's distinctive development. In spite of the break with the Young Catholic Workers, he – like Mother Julia – had no doubt that its different groupings had an important mission to fulfil for the Church: *"We believed in the charism of Catholic Action and regarded it as necessary in rescuing the youth for the Church in the post-war years."* [26] Fr Hillewaere's decision, made in agreement with Mother Julia, did not lead to a break with Canon Cardijn. They remained united in their mutual respect and goodwill.

[24] L. ALAERTS, *Door eigen werk sterk*, p. 526.
[25] *Ibid.*, p. 525.
[26] Letter of Mother Julia, 19 March 1990.

XXII. A new door opens

Throughout her life, Mother Julia sought to discover the traces of God in everyday life, to follow them in the light of faith, and thus to do His Will. With this in mind, she wrote to Fr Hillewaere: *"God holds the way and the plan of The Work in His hands. He rejoices and is glorified, when we seek to comply with His wishes, to do what pleases Him, and to serve Him in dedication and selflessness. In this way our souls grow according to the perfect figure of Christ (see Eph 4:13). Recently I have got so much out of meditating on Jesus with his disciples: Jesus and Peter, Jesus and Judas, the Lord and Paul, our Mother Mary with John and the other disciples."* [1]

The merger of the 'Women's Association of the Christian Worker Movement' and the 'People's Movement for the Family' into a single organisation had led to new problems. Mother Julia and the Sisters recognised that collaboration with the reconstituted organisation would be difficult. It became increasingly clear that the community had to go its own way in the apostolate, in order to be able to realise the aims of the charism, not just in the work with families, but also in its basic direction. She told Fr Hillewaere of her conviction *"that first of all the spiritual life of the Sisters had to be safeguarded"*. [2]

Fr Hillewaere was always a great support to Mother Julia, whatever the situation. On the eve of his 62nd birthday, the twelfth anniversary of the foundation of The Work, she wrote to him: *"Father, it is right that we should thank you for everything you have done and been for us for so many years, for the glorious gift of your priestly life and existence for us. I can find no words to express my profound and devoted thankfulness. Tomorrow at Holy Mass and Communion, united with all the Sisters, we shall meet each other in the heart of Him, Who calls us, and, according to His divine will, has chosen us to be silent witnesses and messengers of His great and merciful love for mankind."* [3]

Mother Julia looked after the young people interested in or preparing

---

[1] Letter of Mother Julia, 7 September 1949.
[2] Letter of Mother Julia, 6 January 1950.
[3] Letter of Mother Julia, 17 January 1950.

to enter the community. She was aware that unity among those who are consecrated has a supernatural influence, which attracts people and opens them up to God. Time and again she reminded the Sisters of the need for this unity: *"My dear Sisters, I ask you out of love for God and for the sake of the grace of our vocation: Love one another in simplicity and sincerity with the supernatural love proper to those who are consecrated to God."* [4]

In spite of her poor health Mother Julia tried to lighten the burden for the Sisters. When she could, she would answer the door or the telephone, and would welcome the people who came to the house with their needs and questions. Various social service organisations from Brussels and the surrounding area made contact with the community, in order to acquaint themselves with the apostolic activity of The Work. However, they sometimes lacked an understanding of the essentials, as Mother Julia recorded: *"We feel such a profound need to strive for unity amongst the works of charity. But we are still far from that spirit, which must be the foundation of this unity. It is not possible to bring peace and unity through the apostolate, if one has not grasped that this demands the way of the cross and of sacrifice and selflessness, as Christ Himself has already shown us by His example."* [5]

She was particularly thankful that there was an opportunity to work with another religious community in Wezembeek. In their new house, the Sisters of The Work lived a more contemplative life and were occupied in various apostolic activities. They cared for families, were involved in catechesis, took on parish duties and helped those who were searching. Mother Julia reported to Fr Hillewaere about the meeting with this religious community: *"We understand each other very well. We have agreed in relation to the parishes on this side of Wezembeek to co-operate in the two activities, working closely together for the same goal: they will take on the care of the sick in their homes and we the work with families."* [6]

The family assistance service in Brussels gradually developed in a new direction. In February 1950 someone else took over some of the important leadership responsibilities in the 'Women's Association of the Christian Worker Movement'. The Sister of The Work, who until then had had much of the responsibility and had achieved much in building up the service, was now working as an administrator. Mother Julia encouraged her not to be disappointed about the way in which this had happened: *"Since the*

[4] Letter of Mother Julia, 22 January 1950.
[5] Letter of Mother Julia, 2 January 1950.
[6] *Ibid.*

Lord ordains it, it is good. We must, it seems to me, accept the consequences of our vocation in His service and for His purposes. I feel and trust that the Lord has taken the running of The Work powerfully in hand." [7]

Her activities in both houses, her concerns for the family service and the guiding of the community cost Mother Julia much of her strength. However, the Lord continually sent her consolation and confidence. She testified: *"Sometimes, I am so tired and exhausted. Nevertheless, I thank Jesus for the difficulties. Sometimes my soul is filled with great joy over the works of the Lord, so that I possess an inner happiness concerning whatever happens and comes our way. How I would like to lead all souls to this assurance! How rich and happy they would be!"* [8]

Mother Julia realised that it was no longer possible to work as before with the family service of the 'Women's Association of the Christian Worker Movement' due to the mounting problems: *"It seems to me that we cannot be involved in this collaboration for much longer. If we have been involved up to now, it is because we did not attempt to anticipate God's plan. Our intention was to serve in the best possible way, and to pass on the light of the charism with this in mind and in this spirit. We are trying to understand each and every person in Christ. I believe that the time has come to witness publicly to the spirit and truth of our vocation in new ways. Though we are as unworthy and undeserving as ever, we hope and trust that with God's help and grace we shall be able to withstand the trials that are coming to The Work, so that it may be sanctified and serve God in His glory."* [9]

In the midst of the joys and difficulties of daily life a new door opened to the further development of the community. In March 1950, Mother Julia was visited by the sister of one of the community, who told her of an unoccupied convent in Villers-Notre-Dame, a village in Wallonia, near Ath. In this village, recorded in documents dating back to 965, a precious statue

Mary, Seat of Wisdom, 12th century

---

[7] Letter of Mother Julia, 22 February 1950.
[8] Letters of Mother Julia, 23 June 1949 and 14 March 1950.
[9] Letter of Mother Julia, 17 March 1950.

The Convent of Villers-Notre-Dame in 1950

of Mary, Seat of Wisdom, which is still revered by the faithful today, had existed since the twelfth century. The village had suffered much damage during the Second World War, and after the war the 'Sisters, Apostles of Saint Joseph' abandoned the convent.

In the following weeks the community prayed for guidance as to whether it was God's will that they should take over the unoccupied convent. For Mother Julia it was not so much a matter of seeking out a new area for their apostolate, but much more a desire to determine whether God was proposing a further development in their work with families and in the progress of the charism. In the middle of April 1950, the decision was reached, with Fr Hillewaere's agreement, to revitalise the abandoned convent.

The community took over the convent, having signed a lease with Count Conrad von Ursel and his wife, who were friends of the Bishop of Tournai. The parish priest of Villers was happy that new life was coming to the parish. They began to clear the site and to undertake the necessary renovations. Mother Julia gave guidance to the Sisters, who moved to Villers, with prayer and advice. She spoke to Fr Hillewaere of their initial experiences: *"There is so much hardship, which we are powerless to face, and yet we are so powerful in Him, who can do everything and who gave his life for the salvation of men. Truly, we must not lose a single instant that Providence sends us in which to serve Him. I constantly entrust to our Mother, Mary, in particular all the activities that we take on for The Work. This gives me so much confidence."* [10]

The inhabitants of the village were very happy that once again consecrated Sisters were moving into the abandoned convent. The Sisters energetically set about making the house habitable, as they wanted to offer children from the city the opportunity to relax in the countryside around Villers during the summer. The people of Villers valued the presence of the community, and, once, when the Sisters had to go to Brussels for a short stay, they impatiently awaited their return. One of the Sisters recalled:

---

[10] Letter of Mother Julia, 12 May 1950.

"The inhabitants of the village were concerned when we went away and did not immediately return. Whenever a train stopped at the station, they would look out for us. After a few days, when we returned, they were so very happy that they placed flowers on our luggage and invited us to pick vegetables. Some of the farmers allowed us to pick cherries." [11]

In the meantime, the house in Brussels had grown too small. There were so many young women interested in the family assistance service that they could no longer all be accommodated in 'St Paul's House' in Ducpétiaux Avenue. As a result the Sisters sought out a new, bigger house in Brussels. They soon found a suitable building in Bollandisten Street, and decided to leave the other house. In April 1950, Mother Julia wrote: *"This week we have signed the lease for the house*

The house of *The Work* in the Bollandisten Street in Brussels

in Bollandisten Street. I have sent the lawyer the contract for legal scrutiny. A benefactress has placed some items at our disposal, which will be useful in furnishing the house." [12] In faithfulness to the word of the Lord: *"Give to Caesar, what belongs to Caesar, and to God, what belongs to God"* (Mt 22:21), Mother Julia was determined that the financial and legal regulations should be properly adhered to, and she and the Sisters continually sought the advice of lay people with the necessary, specialist knowledge.

The new building offered more possibilities for the immediate tasks and their apostolic work. During their training the young assistants lived there alongside the Sisters responsible for them. A welcoming atmosphere prevailed in the house. The peace, cheerfulness and homeliness had a strong, beneficial influence on its inhabitants. The assistants needed to

Reception room

---

[11] Recollections of Mother Julia, written down 1978.
[12] Letter of Mother Julia, 15 April 1950.

experience such an atmosphere for themselves before they could build it up and nurture it in the families, with whom they were to be involved.

Mother Julia wanted the assistants to go through a process of growth that would provide them with the ability to act responsibly and to see things as they really are and not as they wanted them to be. With this in mind, she appealed to the younger generation: *"The sense of responsibility must be anchored in a formed conscience. Every good idea must be able to yield to the objective facts of the case. One can be objective, only if one places oneself and one's personal feelings in the background and surveys and judges the issue in its entirety."* [13] She pointed out that, in providing guidance to other people, empathy and courage to speak the truth had to be combined together: *"Understanding a person does not exclude interfering with their development. Through your intervention, seek not to injure, but to build up."* [14]

Children in the garden of Villers-Notre-Dame

Mother Julia spent most of the summer of 1950 at Villers. The house was bustling with life. Many children came there from Brussels for a break. Mother Julia was fully engaged in the activities and continued to call on the Sisters to persevere in performing their work with love. In the daily fulfilment of duty she saw a way of being redeemed from the consequences of sin and of co-operating with the saving work of Christ. She recognised that the burden of work is light, when it is performed with a joyful, thankful and selfless readiness to serve. For her, the faithful fulfilment of one's duty was essential to overcoming the love of comfort and of self, and to expressing the love of God and of neighbour. She was always aware that all work possessed an apostolic value.

Mother Julia lovingly guided the work of renovation and the education of the children, often from difficult family backgrounds. She explained:

[13] Conversation with Mother Julia, 1954.
[14] *Ibid.*

"At present we have here forty-three children and three mothers with their youngest children as well as three new recruits helping out temporarily. The parish priest has given me a key to the church. It seems to me that the Lord is richly blessing The Work." [15]

As well as the apostolic activity, Mother Julia was concerned to provide spiritual direction to the Sisters, seeking to nurture in their hearts the unity of contemplative attachment to God and loving readiness for service. The division of life into separate areas of religious life and every day work was to her one of the great dangers of our time. For a healthy, spiritual development it was necessary that the light of God should illumine every area of the Sisters' lives and that prayer should bear fruit in the fulfilment of one's duty and in acts of love towards one's neighbour. She returned again and again to this theme: *"Make sure that your prayer and your work are not separated from each other, that every day and every hour your exertions find their echo and expression in prayer. On the other hand, your practical commitment must be the realisation of that which your heart discusses with the Lord in prayer, in the holy sacrifice of the Mass, in the reception of communion, in praying the breviary, in the Stations of the Cross and in other spiritual exercises. In this way, everything will become a reciprocal action of love, an expression of faith, bearing witness to and confessing Him and your existence in Him."* [16]

After the intense activity of the summer months, Mother Julia made sure that the Sisters were given the necessary time for rest and reflection. With this in mind, she turned to Fr Hillewaere: *"We have decided that for the month of September we shall accept no bookings for the house at Villers, so that after the summer months we will have the opportunity for physical and spiritual rest and that we can progress in a good direction – without us becoming overworked through all this activity."* [17]

Fr Hillewaere participated in the development of the community and would occasionally visit them in Villers, since the village was not as far from his parish as Brussels. Just like Mother Julia, he felt that after the initial, challenging period deeper growth was necessary. After one of his visits, Mother Julia wrote: *"I entirely agree with you, Father, that our attention should be directed towards growth in the spirit of our vocation above all else. Regarding this, I have complete confidence when I see how well disposed all the*

[15] Letter of Mother Julia, 4 August 1950.
[16] Letter of Mother Julia, 21 April 1965.
[17] Letter of Mother Julia, 8 September 1950.

Sisters are – without exception. If I think how they have all battled their way through on every level in the last year, I cannot help but sing a Magnificat to the Lord with all my being. Certainly, there is still too much to do. But I am happy about the new opportunities and the increased space, which Providence has so generously given us in the last year. All have had to make great sacrifices, which were bound up with the growth of the community, and brought not a few privations with them. Please pray that the Lord bring everything to a good end and that we all increasingly become instruments in accord with His Heart." [18]

In September 1950, the congress of the Young Catholic Workers took place in Brussels.[19] The congress was attended by an Austrian priest, who, whilst a seminarian, had been sent as a soldier to Flanders in the Second World War, and had met the family of one of the Sisters of The Work whilst there. He used the opportunity to get to know the community, and spent a few days in the house in Bollandisten Street in Brussels. Mother Julia wrote of this visit: *"We had a young priest from Austria as a guest for a few days. He was so very interested in our mission that it is difficult to convey it in words. He said that he knew some young women in his own country, who possessed the same spirit as us. Therefore, he would like to remain in contact with us, if only by letter. He would be glad, if I would consider the possibility of doing something in his country. He seems a very down to earth and spiritual man. I will think about this before the Lord."* [20] This priest from Austria would later become God's instrument for the spread of The Work outside of Belgium.

By now it had become clear that a complete break was necessary with the family assistance service of the 'Women's Association of the Christian Worker Movement' as well as with Catholic Action, and the last of the Sisters involved in this service were withdrawn. The community petitioned the Ministry of Health and the Family for permission to establish their own fully independent family assistance service and for state authorisation to train family assistants. Mother Julia reported to Fr Hillewaere: *"An assessor came yesterday as a result of our application and visit to the Ministry. She appeared sympathetic to the youth work, because it is something new that must surely be developed further. As to the family assistance service, we meet the regulations on all points. If we get authorisation from the Ministry, we become eligible for public funding. I think that it can be useful, if some of our living costs can be met through a guaranteed income. Whilst we carry on the struggle and get on with life, we leave everything*

---

[18] Letter of Mother Julia, 21 October 1950.
[19] Cf. M. Van Roey, *Cardijn*, p. 162.
[20] Letter of Mother Julia, 8 September 1950.

with great confidence to the wonderful, divine guidance of Providence." [21]

After a positive report, the Ministry recognised The Work's independent family assistance service. At the same time the courses for the training of family assistants were also publicly endorsed, and in subsequent years were run from the centre in Bollandisten Street in Brussels and in Villers. The community's work with families did receive state funding, but this was not sufficient to fund the service, and they continued to depend on the help of benefactors.

Mother Julia and Fr Hillewaere saw the family service as an important area of operation for The Work. However, it was clear to them that the community had to remain fundamentally open to all forms of apostolate in the Church. With this in mind, Mother Julia declared: *"It seems to me that The Work has to cultivate and fertilise all the fields in God's vineyard."* [22] Even at that time, she had a good understanding of the approaching religious and social developments, to which the Church would have to discern its response: *"It is a matter of responding to the needs of the times, to the new paganism and the decline of faith. Our time is faced with centralisation and internationalisation in every area of life. The Church must react to this development."* [23]

With regard to the external forms that apostolic activity should take, religious dynamism and openness to the signs of divine Providence were needed, in order to be able to respond to new developments in faithfulness to the charism

Youngsters in Villers-Notre-Dame

of The Work. Mother Julia declared to Fr Hillewaere: *"It seems as if the Lord wants me to understand in regard to the development of The Work that we must not place too much significance on the external forms that The Work currently assumes."* [24] She did not want to call into question the importance of the family service with these words, but rather to draw attention to the fact that the work with children, young people and families was only one of many possible forms

---

[21] Letter of Mother Julia, 4 October 1950.
[22] Letter of Mother Julia, 10 July 1949.
[23] Letter of Mother Julia, 10 July 1948.
[24] Letter of Mother Julia, 20 June 1950.

of apostolic activity in The Work. According to its particular mission the community had to remain open to other activities, in order to be able to respond to the Church's different needs.

Mother Julia was very pleased, when in the autumn of 1950, alongside the work of caring for families, another development occurred in Villers. People asked if they could come for days of recollection. Priests from the area contacted them about going to Villers for periods of silent retreat. Youth groups spent days of rest in the house, deepening their faith.

The particular path that The Work had pursued in the family service, and the developments bound up with it, filled Mother Julia with thankfulness and a great inner peace. From its foundation in 1938, The Work had evolved in accordance with God's dispensation in the sphere of Catholic Action in Belgium. Up until this time, Mother Julia and the young community sought to co-operate in the renewal and spiritual development of various groups within Catholic Action with the charism of The Work. In 1950 they started out in a direction that was completely independent of Catholic Action. Now The Work was like a spring of fresh water carving out its own river bed.

The independent path taken by The Work was also influenced by developments in Catholic Action in Belgium. In the years after the Second World War, relations among various groups within the movement, especially within the Young Catholic Workers, had grown increasingly strained. The international congress, held in Brussels in September 1950 on the theme, 'A new spirit is going through the land',[25] was to become a new highpoint, and to demonstrate publicly the success of the Young Catholic Workers.[26] At this congress the new spirit of the movement was made clear: *"It is no longer a question of the dangers arising from a new paganism or from a de-Christianised world"*,[27] but of the general good of young workers.[28] The role of people in the working environment was no longer to be interpreted in the light of the Gospel, as had been the case before, but rather in terms of its social and collective significance. This one-sided direction was a cause of concern to many people. Even Pope Pius XII spoke in a radio talk to the participants at the congress of the dangers of a kind of class ideology.[29]

Canon Cardijn was worried by these developments, which weighed on

---

[25] L. ALAERTS, *Door eigen werk sterk*, p. 406.

[26] Cf. *ibid.*, pp. 405-407.

[27] *Ibid.*, p. 408.

[28] Cf. *ibid.*, pp. 406-408.

[29] Pius XII, 'Radio message to Young Christian Workers, Brussels, Sept. 3, 1950' in *Acta Apostolicae Sedis*, 42 (1950) 639-642, esp. 640-641; cf. ALAERTS, *Door eigen werk sterk*, p. 408.

his conscience, and later expressed his concerns openly: *"The future of the Young Catholic Workers! Everyone will understand that, in my old age, I am more anxious about it than others. The many questions that are decisive for the future can frighten a person. Amongst these problems are to be counted, it seems to me, internal contradictions and external difficulties. Humanly speaking there is no solution."* [30] In spite of these problems Cardijn tirelessly promoted the realisation of the aims of his movement on an international level, whilst calling for loyalty to the Church.[31] Pope Paul VI made him a Cardinal in 1965 in recognition of his lifelong commitment to young workers.[32]

Mother Julia and Fr Hillewaere had to take the young community of The Work in a direction different in some respects to that of Catholic Action. It was not to be a mass movement, but a spiritual family, which was to contribute to the spiritual renewal of the people of God and to the building up of the Mystical Body of Christ. For them it was not primarily a humanitarian and social matter, but above all a matter of a living faith, permeating every area of life, of unity conforming to Jesus's prayer in the Upper Room, and of a sincere love for the Church. In Mother Julia's heart there burnt a desire to give herself unconditionally to the Lord, so that He would guide The Work safely along this path. She wrote: *"I was filled with a great zeal to sacrifice myself for the development of The Work. I am absolutely certain that The Work is God's will and is supported by Him."* [33]

---

[30] M. FIEVEZ and J. MEERT, *Cardijn*, p. 174.
[31] Cf. *ibid.*
[32] Cf. *ibid.*, p. 173.
[33] Letter of Mother Julia, 10 October 1949.

XXIII. The arrival of the Eucharistic Lord

An unexpected telephone call was received from Count Conrad von Ursel in the house at Villers in the summer of 1950. He announced that the Bishop of Tournai was with him and would like to visit the revitalised house and to get to know the community better. Mother Julia and the Sisters were in the process of preparing lunch for the many children who were staying with them in Villers at this time. Before they had had time to prepare a proper welcome, Bishop Charles-Marie Himmer was standing at the door with the Count. He was pleased to meet Mother Julia and the community, marvelling at the work they were doing with the children, and was impressed by the newly refurbished house.

Mother Julia took the Bishop and his secretary to the chapel. For many years the Blessed Sacrament had not been reserved in the tabernacle. Since their arrival in the convent the Sisters had used the chapel as an oratory. Thinking that the Lord was present in the tabernacle, the bishop immediately genuflected and removed his purple zucchetto.[1] Mother Julia turned to him respectfully and said: *"Your Excellency, you do not need to genuflect or take off your pileolus. The Lord does not dwell in this tabernacle. But it is within your power to grant us this grace, which we long for so much!"* [2] The secretary accompanying him nodded supportively, and the bishop encouraged Mother Julia to put her request in writing.

Mother Julia wrote immediately to the bishop asking for permission, and on 27 September 1950 received the following reply from his secretary: *"The*

Bishop Charles-Marie Himmer

---

[1] A bishop's skull-cap, also called a 'pileolus'.
[2] Recollections of Mother Julia, written down 22 April 2003.

bishop has very fond memories of his visit. He was impressed by the neatness of the house as well as the joy and great love that prevailed there. He is happy to grant your request to reserve the Blessed Sacrament in your chapel. He knows that the presence of the Lord will be a great comfort to you and that you will continue to maintain your presence in the parish." [3] Mother Julia, Fr Hillewaere and the entire community rejoiced and gave thanks at their request being granted. For the three years of common life they had shared together, they had longed for the day when the Eucharistic Lord would dwell amongst them.

Mother Julia had possessed a spiritual bond with the Eucharist from her childhood, receiving daily strength from the Sacrifice of the Mass and Holy Communion. She experienced a profound sense of wonder at the presence of the Lord in the Sacrament of the Altar. At the Sacrifice of the Mass she would constantly renew her commitment to God: *"I feel incapable of expressing the sublime idea of the Eucharistic presence of the Lord. I lose myself in Him like a drop of water in a great ocean."* [4] It was through the Holy Eucharist that she received many of the graces that were bound up with the foundation and the development of the community. She possessed the strong belief that The Work grows through the Eucharist, just as the entire Church is permanently animated and renewed through the mystery of the Body and Blood of Christ. In a letter to one of the Sisters, she testified to this belief in the following manner: *"Christ is the head of The Work, whose members we are without distinction. In Him we have a mission to fulfil, arising from within, in the great body of the Church. All the consecrated are called to be love in this body in a sublime manner – sublime and simple at the same time. Everything is simple in Christ, our friend and brother. Yet, how inclined we are to make the simplest things difficult and complicated. 'If you do not become like children, you cannot enter the Kingdom of Heaven'* (Mt 18:3). *This Kingdom is simplicity, peace and joy from the Father, the Son and the Holy Spirit. I pray that the three divine Persons may dwell in you more and more. Ask for this every morning in Holy Communion or when you visit a Church or Chapel. Then for a moment observe Jesus and listen to Him in His obedience."* [5]

Whilst daily life continued in the community and they fulfilled their apostolic duties with love and devotion, Mother Julia and the Sisters

[3] Letter of Mgr J. Hachez, Bishop's secretary, Diocese of Tournai (Belgium), 27 September 1950.
[4] Letter of Mother Julia, 3 February 1949.
[5] Letter of Mother Julia, 12 June 1960.

waited with joy for the arrival of the Eucharistic King. The first Mass in the chapel was scheduled for the eve of the Solemnity of All Saints.

Mother Julia was fully conscious of the great significance of this day for the further development of The Work, and wanted very much that the Sisters should not only undertake the necessary external preparations for this day, but should learn to see it as a landmark in the history of the community. It was at this time that she wrote the following letter to all the Sisters.

October 1950

Beloved Sisters!

In these final days of preparation for the great event, which The Work awaits, I feel I must write a word or two to you all, in order to share my inner joy and gratitude in the Lord.

It must surely fill us all with joy and gratitude that in a few days time we shall celebrate the joyful arrival of the good Master into our midst at the first Sacrifice of the Mass. It is a day of great significance for The Work, a day which we have awaited in silence and for which we have yearned so much, until the Lord could no longer resist the great trust that we have placed in Him.

Dear Sisters, as we make the preparations here, to welcome the divine Bridegroom worthily, my thoughts go out to you all the time. I pray that the outward activity with its troubles and demands may also help to lay the firm foundations in the soul of every one of you of the apostolic virtues and the love of sacrifice, which are the necessary guarantees of the future of The Work. The Lord seems to be looking with pleasure on the sacrifice that every one of you has made.

Fr Hillewaere is permitting us, in this first Holy Mass, to offer ourselves anew with a deeper consciousness to Christ the King, and to give ourselves completely for His Kingdom in souls and in the world. Do this by placing yourselves in the hands of Mary, the Mother of God.

Think constantly in these final days, which precede the feast of Christ the King and our first Holy Mass, of the grace of your vocation and of your being chosen. Lift your eyes above this material world in its misery so that you may meet the gaze of Christ and His will may become the nourishment of your life. This will happen, if your intentions are pure and your will is free of all unruly desires and any self-interest. Fr Hillewaere will be united with us, celebrating Holy Mass on the same day at the same time.

May we all become more deeply one through the grace of the 'Holy Covenant', just as the Father is in the Son and the Son is in the Father and we are in Them. Let us ask for this from the Lord especially during these days. He is almighty!

May God bless you all.

Joined in profound unity, Mother Julia[6]

Before the arrival of the Eucharistic Lord, the Sisters held a Triduum beginning with the Solemnity of Christ the King, which was celebrated on the last Sunday in October at that time. The Sisters also used this period as an opportunity to prepare themselves through prayer, reflection and study for the proclamation of the dogma of the bodily Assumption of Mary into heaven. On the eve of the feast of Christ the King, the parish priest of Villers had already brought the Blessed Sacrament for a Holy Hour in the community's chapel. This increased the Sisters' longing for the permanent presence of the Lord. Mother Julia testified: *"We yearn for the Eucharistic presence of the Lord amongst us. I expect so much from it. Sometimes I am overwhelmed by the nearness of God. My experience is that my soul loves the Lord, and the Lord loves my soul."* [7]

Monstrance in the house chapel in Villers-Notre-Dame

The Mass on the last day of the Triduum was prepared with great care. In spite of its simplicity the chapel radiated a festive atmosphere. The necessary sacred objects had been made ready in accordance with Church regulations. Mother Julia always treated the Holy as holy. She realised the beneficial and sanctifying influence of the sacred on human nature. She expected preparation and celebration of the liturgy in a way that was appropriate to the sacred character of the divine mysteries and would nurture a healthy

---

[6] Circular Letter of Mother Julia, October 1950.

[7] Letter of Mother Julia, 23 October 1950.

spiritual life. So she put all her energy into creating a sacred atmosphere in the chapel, in which souls in the midst of their daily routine could more easily raise themselves up to God. Fr Hillewaere's help and advice was much sought after during the preparations. It was a great sacrifice both for him and the community that he could not be present at the first Mass on account of his parish duties in the lead up to the Solemnity of All Saints. However, he expressed his joy at the approaching event in a letter: *"It is of great importance that you have been allowed to reserve the Lord in the chapel at Villers. It proves that*

House chapel in Villers-Notre-Dame, October 1950

the Bishop of Tournai trusts The Work and its spirit. This is of great significance for the history of The Work. Celebrate this Mass in thankfulness for all the graces received!" [8]

The 1 November 1950 was a historic day in the history of the Church on account of the proclamation of the dogma of the bodily Assumption of Mary into heaven. On the previous day the parish priest of Villers had celebrated the Holy Sacrifice of the Mass in the chapel for the first time with the whole of the community. All the Sisters from the various locations tried to be present at the celebration, in which the Eucharistic Lord took residence for the first time in one of the houses of The Work. In gratitude they sang the hymn, *'Christus vincit, Christus regnat, Christus imperat'*, and a heartfelt *'Te Deum'*!

Now Christ was even more the centre of the young community. From now on the Sisters would gather together again and again before the tabernacle to praise and glorify the Lord, to obtain the strength to fulfil their apostolic duties, and to bring the many needs of the Church and the world to Him. Mother Julia was very touched by the fact that she had been permitted to live under the same roof as the Blessed Sacrament. She informed one Sister: *"I have to be alone for a short time to reflect on The Work and its developing life. It is restful and pleasant here. Dear Sister, it is encouraging to know that only a thin wall separates me from His Eucharistic presence. We – Jesus and I – are mindful*

---

[8] Letter of Fr Hillewaere to Mother Julia, October 1950.

of and love everything that the Father wills and holds dear. Ah, I cannot say how glorious our impressive chapel is, and how much it draws and inspires me. What a great blessing!" [9]

Throughout her life, love for the Eucharist compelled her to lead those entrusted to her care to this unique source of grace: *"He lives with us under one roof, and shares our daily life through his obedient and hidden dwelling amongst us in the chapel. There is His living presence in Eucharistic form, providing a light, model and life-giving force for us. Go quickly to Him in spirit in every stressful situation, with every doubt and in every experience. Lay all before Him, and leave it to Him! In this way you will become one with Him, the solitary, obedient, waiting and watching Lord Jesus!"* [10]

In 1934, Christ the King, crowned with thorns, had drawn Mother Julia to Himself with the bonds of love in a 'Holy Covenant'. With divine power, He guided the development of the charism according to His wonderful plan. In her later years, Mother Julia bore witness to her faith in Christ the King's guidance of The Work with the following words: *"Not only at the beginning of The Work, but through all the years of growth, He has shown Himself as the King, Who never ceases to stand by his little flock. He never ceases to draw us lovingly to an ever purer, stronger, more devoted and more fruitful love for the sake of His Kingdom, which is in such need. He has called us, so that through us the joy of salvation may be disseminated in the most beautiful homage to His grace and mercy. Through our faithful commitment and our obedience to the holy will of God, through our selfless devotion and love, which co-operates in the restoration of His Kingdom, unity in righteousness and peace is forged."* [11] Mother Julia always possessed a confident belief that Christ, the King crowned with thorns, remained with His own in the Holy Eucharist, nourishing, strengthening and binding them together in unity. She regarded love for the Holy Eucharist as a pre-eminent expression of love for the Church.

Mother Julia was a thoroughly Eucharistic soul. God's wonderful Providence ordained that she should pass away on 29 August 1997 – a Friday, whilst her spiritual sons and daughters celebrated Holy Mass in the Church of the Convent of Thalbach in Bregenz and some of them prayed at her sickbed. The Lord called her to her eternal home during the consecration,

---

[9] Letter of Mother Julia, December 1950.
[10] Letter of Mother Julia, August 1970.
[11] Mother Julia's Notes, 18 October 1982.

at which, throughout her whole life, she had offered herself up with Jesus for The Work and for the intentions of the entire Church. Several years before her death she expressed the wish that the following words should be written on her tombstone: *"God's merciful and just love seeks you, watches over you, and waits for you. Go to Him in the Holy Eucharist!"* [12]

During her life, Mother Julia emphasised again and again that Jesus Christ had founded The Work for the sake of the Church, and wanted her to be His pliant instrument and bride. She often stressed that the Lord, present in the Blessed Sacrament, would protect and guide The Work in the midst of all its joys and difficulties. In her reverence for God's plan and in her humble trust

Mother Julia's tomb in the Convent of Thalbach, in Bregenz, Austria

in His unswerving faithfulness, she wanted to be and to remain a model for those who are called. With this in mind she summed up the mission of her life in the following words: *"Always be aware of what is important: not my person, but the shining light and the special nature of the vocation, the doctrine of the Mystical Body of Christ, the mutual complementarity of gifts and graces that Christ has ordained for the Church, His Bride. I am merely a channel of his just and merciful love for humanity in these times."* [13]

---

[12] Circular Letter of Mother Julia, 19 March 1991.
[13] Conversation with Mother Julia, 25 August 1994.

Appendices

Afterword – a brief overview of the later development of The Work

This book about Mother Julia and the origins of The Spiritual Family The Work ends with the arrival of the Blessed Sacrament in the chapel at Villers. This event gave Mother Foundress much strength and confidence concerning the future progress of The Work and remained fixed in her memory. Looking back many years later, she wrote to one of the Sisters: *"This day in 1950 was for The Work the day, on which the King of kings entered His Work. In this way He set the seal on His dwelling amongst us. How thankful we must be for this favour!"* [1] Towards the end of her life, she testified with great emotion: *"On this day we were filled as it were with new life, with newly awakened life on our pilgrim way."* [2]

The full story of Mother Julia's continuing journey along her pilgrim way, which is bound up inseparably with the growth and expansion of the community, requires further careful research and awaits completion at a later time. Here, we simply wish to outline some of the steps in the further development of The Work, in order to bring events up to date. The community's development shows how truly the words of Jesus were fulfilled in Mother Julia's commitment: *"If the seed does not fall to the ground and die, it remains alone. But if it dies, it brings forth rich fruit"* (Jn 12:24). The charism of The Work is a gift of God for our time, as well as the fruit of Mother Julia's commitment. From the little sapling of the charism, the beginnings of which are described in this book, there has grown a sturdy tree, which has spread its roots into many countries.

From the outset, Mother Julia considered it very important to keep the relevant Church authorities informed about The Work. When he was seventy years old Fr Hillewaere was relieved of his duties as a parish priest, and was able to retire to the house in Villers-Notre-Dame with the permission of his bishop, Mgr Emiel-Jozef De Smedt, in order to help the growing community. Mother Julia took this opportunity to approach the

---

[1] Letter of Mother Julia, 30 October 1977.
[2] Letter of Mother Julia, 1 May 1992.

Bishop of Tournai about establishing The Work as a '*Pia Unio*' ('Pious Union'). On 17 January 1959, Bishop Charles-Marie Himmer granted this ecclesiastical recognition with a view to a later establishment of The Work as a community of consecrated life.

With the grace imparted by the episcopal recognition, the community spread beyond Belgium in the following years. In 1963, some members were sent to Innsbruck, where, with the consent of Bishop Paul Rusch, the first centre in Austria was founded. From Innsbruck other communities were founded in Vienna and Munich. In 1965, the first Sisters went to Rome to live the vocation in the heart of the Church. In subsequent years further centres were established in several countries in eastern and western Europe, as well as in Jerusalem. Members of The Work are also active in other continents.

It was a great loss to Mother Julia and the community, when Fr Hillewaere was called to his eternal home on 3 January 1972. Right up until his death he had guided the development of The Work with great faith and quiet devotion. Some years later, God ordained that Fr Philip Boyce OCD, Professor of Dogmatics and Spirituality in Rome, and since 1995 bishop of his home diocese of Raphoe in Ireland, was to become the spiritual director of Mother Julia and The Work.

In the years after 1970 the community of priests began to take concrete shape. Various priests heard the call to perform their pastoral ministry in the spirit of The Work. Some young men, who were preparing for the priesthood, experienced the invitation to offer themselves up completely for the charism and to serve the Church in unity with the Sisters in accordance with the principles of The Work. On 4 August 1986, the Priests' Community was officially established by Bishop Bruno Wechner of Feldkirch and united with the 'Pious Union' of the Sisters' community. In the following years, The Work began to undertake the formation of its own priests in the 'Collegium Paulinum' in Rome. As well as the centre in Rome, there are now houses of the Priests' Community in several countries.

The members of The Work do not follow any particular apostolate, and neither do they exclude any. They wish to stand ready to meet the needs of the Church, and to work in the spirit of their charism, wherever God's Providence should happen to lead them. They are involved in pastoral, social, educational and cultural work in all levels of society, seeking to co-operate in the great task of the new evangelisation.

Over time the charism of The Work has developed like a tree with a single trunk and two sturdy branches: the Sisters' community and the Priests' Community, to which priests, deacons, brothers and fratres (men preparing for Holy Orders) belong. These members in the strict sense form the core of The Work and promise to live the three evangelical counsels: virginal love, evangelical poverty and loving obedience. Closely bound to the two main branches are many other smaller branches, which also belong to The Work. Amongst these are the members in a wider sense, who are also called co-operators: bishops, priests, deacons, seminarians of different dioceses; married couples and families; single people and those who are widowed. They enter into a 'Holy Covenant' in a form appropriate to their position in life, and strive to live out the grace of the charism, wherever their activities and obligations take them. In addition there are the faithful, who are spiritually united to The Work, either through consecration to the Sacred Heart of Jesus and the blessing of their homes or through the 'Evening Blessing', which has created a community of prayer and blessing that has spread across all the continents.

Mother Julia supported the interior and exterior growth of The Work through her motherly love, her prayer and sacrifice, as well as her counsel and her clear guidance. She regarded it as the great mission of her life to guide the further development of the charism and the expansion of her spiritual family, and to sacrifice herself to this task. The experience of this slow, organic development brought her great joy. She was extremely happy to be permitted in her last years to see the development of all the branches on the tree of The Work that God had ordained for the charism from the beginning.

From early on Mother Julia recognised that The Work was meant for the universal Church and not for one or two dioceses, and that it involved a new form of consecrated life. She wished to wait patiently for the Church to approve such new forms of consecrated life before applying for papal recognition. This became possible after the publication of the new Code of Canon Law in 1983 and the subsequent synod of bishops on the consecrated life in 1994.

Now the time had come to request papal recognition. Mother Julia followed with great interest and encouragement the work of the different members preparing for this under the direction of those internationally responsible for the Priests' and Sisters' Communities. Right up until her death on 29 August 1997, she was confident that the Church would recognise the charism of The Work, just as she had received it from God. Mother Julia's last earthly resting place is in the church of the Convent of Thalbach in Bregenz, the most important house of the community in Austria.

On 11 June 1999, the Solemnity of the Most Sacred Heart of Jesus, Cardinal Camillo Ruini recognised and established The Work as a new form of consecrated life in the diocese of Rome, where the community had had its headquarters since 1993. Two years later on 29 August 2001, The Work received papal recognition as a 'Family of Consecrated Life'. It is probably no coincidence that this highest form of ecclesiastical recognition by the Holy Father happened on the fourth anniversary of the death of the foundress. It would appear that through this providential dispensation God wished to demonstrate once again the truth of the words that Mother Julia left her spiritual sons and daughters:

> *"In heaven I shall remain*
> *what I was for you on earth,*
> *a Mother for all of you.*
> *For this is a gift that God has placed in my heart.*
> *And what God gives, endures forever."* [3]

---

[3] Conversation with Mother Julia, 23 August 1994.

Papal Approval

CONGREGATION
FOR INSTITUTES OF CONSECRATED LIFE
AND SOCIETIES OF APOSTOLIC LIFE

Prot. No. MR. 1 – 1/99

DECREE

The Spiritual Family The Work ("Het Werk"), composed of a Priests' Community and a Community of Consecrated Women, was founded in Belgium on 18 January 1938, at that time the Feast of the Chair of Saint Peter the Apostle, by Miss Julia Verhaeghe, it being the fruit of her surrender to Christ the King, crowned with thorns, and of her love for Mother Church. The core of The Work is made up of the members in the narrow sense who consecrate themselves to God through *a Holy Covenant with the Sacred Heart of Jesus* in the three evangelical counsels. There are also those who are members in the broad sense and other faithful who are spiritually united with them.

The *Community of Consecrated Women* was erected as a Pious Union on 17 January 1959 by His Excellency, Most Rev. Charles-Marie Himmer, Bishop of Tournai, while the *Priests' Community* was officially recognized and joined to the *Community of Consecrated Women* on 4 August 1986 by His Excellency, Most Rev. Bruno Wechner, Bishop of Feldkirch, with a view to the future ecclesiastical approbation of The Work as an Institute of Consecrated Life.

On 11 June 1999, the Solemnity of the Sacred Heart of Jesus, after a period of maturation of its Charism and its diffusion in numerous dioceses, Cardinal Camillo Ruini, Vicar General of His Holiness for the Diocese of Rome, by the authority received from the Congregation for Institutes of Consecrated Life and Societies of Apostolic Life, recognized The Spiritual Family The Work as an Institute of Consecrated Life of Diocesan Right.

The purpose of The Work is to be a reflection of the mystery of the Church, in praise of the Holy Trinity and for the salvation of souls, and to give witness to its supernatural beauty as the Body of Christ and the Family of God. Rooted in the Holy Eucharist, the source of unity with God and with each other, and in fidelity to the Successor of Peter and to the sound doctrine of the Faith, the members seek to help people to more profoundly understand the mystery of the Church and to be strengthened in love for her in view of the signs of the times. In their contemplative and apostolic vocation, and in their mission of sanctifying the world, the members follow above all the example of St Paul, imitating his love for the Lord and his Body, the Church. As spiritual fathers and mothers, they also look with confidence to the Holy Family of Nazareth as the true model of unity and complementarity.

His Holiness, Pope John Paul II, having heard the favorable opinion of the Congregation for Institutes of Consecrated Life and Societies of Apostolic Life, approved The Work as a Family of Consecrated Life.

Therefore, the same Dicastery, with this Decree, declares that The Spiritual Family The Work is a Family of Consecrated Life of Pontifical Right and, consequently, establishes that it is to be recognized as such by all.

At the same time, the text of its Constitutions, written in German, a copy of which is kept in the Archives of this Congregation, are approved and confirmed for a period of ten years.

May the members of the above-mentioned Family of Consecrated Life live their vocation with faith, hope and charity, participating with generosity in the work of Redemption and, faithful to their particular Charism and guided by the Blessed Virgin Mary, may they be a living witness to the Gospel in the world today.

All things to the contrary notwithstanding.

From the Vatican, 29 August 2001, the Fourth Anniversary of the death of Mother Foundress Julia Verhaeghe.

Eduardo Card. Martinez Somalo
Prefect

Mons. Juan J. Dorronsoro
Undersecretary

POPE JOHN PAUL II

Words of welcome to the members
of The Spiritual Family The Work
at the Audience of 10 November 2001

Dear sisters and brothers of The Spiritual Family The Work,

With great joy I greet you at this audience and am happy that a meeting with this new Family of Consecrated Life is possible. At the beginning of a new century you are standing before a great challenge: people today are looking for men and women who show them Jesus Christ. Through your high ideals and youthful enthusiasm you strive to make yourselves, so to speak, the index finger for Jesus. Therefore I have granted you my approval.

Your community can be very useful precisely in the old continent of Europe, because our contemporaries listen to convinced Christians who let themselves be bound and sent by God. Concerning this the foundress of your spiritual family, Mother Julia, gives you a beautiful saying to help you on your way: "*Since Jesus Christ founded the Church everything has been founded. It is only necessary that people live this foundation profoundly.*"

That you may profoundly fulfill your calling for the praise of God and the salvation of souls I gladly give you my Apostolic Blessing.

POPE JOHN PAUL II

Message to The Spiritual Family The Work

Dear sisters and brothers of The Spiritual Family The Work,

1. In the joyous community of the Triune God, the Father and the Son and the Holy Spirit, I send you my heartfelt greetings and best wishes. Your joy over the approval of your Spiritual Family moves you to give renewed witness to your solidarity with the Successor of Peter and your readiness to serve him. I gladly thank Christ, the Lord of the Church, with you for the charism bestowed on you and pray that it may bring forth rich fruit.

2. In the spirit of your foundress you are determined to meet the challenges of our times in the strength of the Catholic Faith. It is given to you to joyfully serve the Church and mankind as a contemplative and, at the same time, apostolic community, which seeks to work as leaven in the world. You have generously accepted the invitation of the Lord to get "to work" for his kingdom. If you remain always available for the plan of God and put your talents at the service of the salvific mission of the Church, your Spiritual Family can become a powerful instrument of the new evangelization, especially in Europe. Your lived surrender to God is the best answer to the urgent questions of mankind and to the needs of the times.

3. In dialogue with the Father, Jesus summarized his salvific mission: "*I glorified you on earth, having accomplished the work which you gave me to do*" (Jn 17:4). The work of Christ – the glorification of God and the redemption of mankind – is continued by the Church in the power of the Holy Spirit through all times. Your Spiritual Family is born from the Church. As members of The Work you are ready to make the mission of the Church of Christ your own.

4. The Church is the great work of God. If her divine origin is questioned at times today, The Work contributes to the understanding and living of the mystery of the Church in its profundity. Remain faithful to the aim of

your Community: be a reflection of the Church to the praise of the Triune God and for the salvation of mankind. Bear witness to the beauty of the Church as the People of God, the Bride of Christ and the Temple of the Holy Spirit. Remain always deeply rooted in the Holy Eucharist, the source of unity with God and with each other.

5. The spirit of adoration is alive in your Community. God is in the centre: your thoughts and deeds revolve around Him. In this way The Work can be an effective instrument against resignation, which also sometimes overcomes the servants of the Church. May your prayer and action in the great work of God bear fruit for the salvation of mankind! May the Lord of history guide the way of your Spiritual Family into the future. I heartily impart to you my Apostolic Blessing.

The Vatican, 10 November 2001

PHILIP BOYCE, OCD

Homily at the Mass of Thanksgiving for the Papal Approval of The Spiritual Family The Work

11 November 2001

One day in conversation, Mother Julia said: *"If love is not in the heart, gratitude will not be on our lips."* [1] It is one of those "sayings" of wisdom which she did not write but speak, and which a living tradition will hand down.

It is that love for Christ, our Saviour and King, and for his holy Church that brings us together in such large numbers from many lands to give thanks for the Papal approval of The Spiritual Family The Work. This is a very significant grace, for which it is right to give thanks. Our Mother Julia would certainly have done so, as she surely does now in the light of Eternity.

During the drafting of the Constitutions, Mother Julia wrote: *"I am able to contemplate the wonderful beauty and power with which our Mother the Church is endowed, and the springs of life that gush forth from her and flow over all God's works and sacraments...This contemplation gives me an inner strength which fills me to overflowing with gratitude for the inexpressible favours with which He fills our life."* [2] How much more so would she give thanks for the gift we are now celebrating?

The grace we have received implies that we recall the vocation we have been given and that we increase our efforts to live it faithfully. Twenty-two years ago to the day, on her birthday, Mother Julia recalled the many graces received during her life and affirmed that among them all *"the grace of her vocation"* stood out as a pre-eminent sign of God's mercy and goodness to her. Each member of The Work I am sure would also acknowledge what a precious grace it has been to know this Charism and to belong to our Spiritual Family.

Every privilege, however, brings with it a corresponding responsibility.

---

[1] Recollections of Mother Julia, written down 11 November 2001.
[2] Letter of Mother Julia, 28 November 1985.

The vocation demands a life of deep faith, an ongoing conversion of heart to God, undaunted confidence in a providential design that guides our ways, a life of virtue, prayer and sacrifice. This has to be lived in a spirit of love and humility, endeavouring at all times to strive for unity and to make every effort to be, like the early Christians, *"one heart and one soul"* (Acts 4:32) in the bonds of peace.

The Crown of Thorns which is on the crest of The Work symbolizes the willingness of its members to enter with Christ their King into the toil and sorrow of the work of redemption. It invites them unceasingly as the Constitutions say *"to live, in union with their Lord and King, an irreproachable life in humility and in fidelity to their vocation"*.

The Papal approval just received will bind each member of The Work more directly to the Holy Father, the Vicar of Christ. We must be more willing than ever, within the grace of our vocation, to obey and to venture on his word. In his Apostolic Letter, *Novo Millennio Ineunte*, he has called us all to put out into deep waters and to pay out our nets for a catch (Lk 5:4). *"Duc in altum! Let us go forward in hope! A new millennium is opening before the Church like a vast ocean upon which we shall venture, relying on the help of Christ."*[3]

Mother Julia spoke of the need of apostolic virtues and self-sacrificing love. This will be the peculiar force of The Work, an influence that comes as much from what we are as from what we do. As the Constitutions state: *"The members of The Work must be sustained by the conviction that, by means of their purified conscience, they have an apostolic influence that can invite and direct those whose heart is open for the truth."* And quoting Mother Julia, they continue: *"A conscience, that repeatedly follows God in the concrete situations of daily life, will shine out because it is turned to God, who is Light (cf. Jn 1:5). It will shine out, because the heart is no longer afraid of sacrifice since it loves with sincerity and not simply with words and mere talk, but in deed and in truth (cf. I Jn 3:18.)."*

My brothers and sisters, be not afraid. As the Spirit led our Mother Foundress and the first generation of Sisters, so will this same Spirit lead us today and always. If we could be brought back to the early post-war years when as yet there was no Priests' Community, no foundations outside Belgium and no Constitutions, we would surely be tempted to doubt how The Work as an international Community of Consecrated Life could ever obtain the highest approval of Pontifical Right. For more than five decades

---

[3] John Paul II, Apostolic Letter *Novo Millennio Ineunte*, No. 58.

this new form of Consecrated Life has stood the test. Finally, what Mother wrote already in 1939 became a reality: *"Rome stands before my eyes. The Holy Father must give his blessing to The Work."* [4]

Mother Julia and the first Sisters at that time felt that there was nothing with them at that time but the grace of God. Then she was given the thought: but what if all use their different gifts and talents, not against each other or isolated from each other but complementing each other? And this truth of "complementarity" has produced much fruit over the years. *"Even though the skies are dark and thundery and the seas are storm-tossed, the Lord and Master is on board of the boat as He once was with his disciples. He is the hope and assurance of those who have taken their place in the boat."* [5]

Away back in 1950 as we heard from the letter quoted earlier on, Mother Julia asked the members of The Work to raise their eyes above earthly things *"to meet Christ's eyes"* so that his will become their daily bread. Again, the present Holy Father, Pope John Paul II, in his Apostolic Letter, *Novo Millennio Ineunte,* has asked us all to look towards the face of Christ. We can take these words as addressed to each one of us: *"Our witness would be hopelessly inadequate if we ourselves had not first contemplated his face [...] . One can never really reach Jesus except by the path of faith [...] . We cannot come to the fullness of contemplation of the Lord's face by our own efforts alone, but by allowing grace to take us by the hand and by the experience of silence and prayer."* [6]

This will encourage us to be faithful at all times to that essential element of our vocation, namely prayer and adoration before the Blessed Sacrament. There, in faith, we shall contemplate the face of Christ and be nourished for our daily life in fidelity to the Charism we have received.

And do everything in union with Our Lady, Seat of Wisdom and Cause of Our Joy. Let her lead you by the hand and keep you near to her Divine Son.

Mother Julia once said about fifty years ago: *"We must give the Lord the most beautiful thing we have."* [7] What more beautiful than our own life through which the love we receive from his Sacred Heart returns to Him in a life of fidelity to the vocation and to the Constitutions that have been approved by the Church. For, as the final words of the Constitutions have

---

[4] Letter of Mother Julia, 18 April 1939.
[5] Letter of Mother Julia, 11 November 1989.
[6] John Paul II, Apostolic Letter *Novo Millennio Ineunte*, Nos. 16, 19, 20.
[7] Recollections of Mother Julia, written down 11 November 2001.

it, the more these Constitutions permeate the lives of the members of The Work, *"the more will they comply with the Lord's request that 'they may all be one', the more will they bear witness to the beauty of the Church and be able to put themselves at the service of God's plan 'ad laudem et gloriam Dei' – 'for God's honour and glory.'"* And the Constitutions end with the words: *"Fidelity is dedicated love."* [8] Amen.

---

[8] Conversation with Mother Julia, 1973.

LEO CARDINAL SCHEFFCZYK

Meeting Mother Julia
Extracts from a Testimony[1]

The author's first meeting with Mother Julia Verhaeghe goes back to
the early eighties, during his first visit to the community in Bregenz.
At that time, Mother Foundress was already in a very weakened state of
health, and thereafter she never fully recovered. That is why, with a few
exceptions, subsequent visits took place by her sickbed. They happened at
regular, roughly six-monthly intervals, which provided the opportunity
for numerous conversations with a woman who, though physically ill,
was mentally alert. A luminous power, still perceptible in the noble and
refined features of her face, shone out of her.

The very first meeting left the impression of an attractive gentleness and
kindness of character, communicated in Mother Julia's face and words.
Also evident was her extraordinary mental capacity for recollection and
concentration, which was the source of a multitude of spiritual thoughts
and considerations. In fact, the conversations were almost exclusively
spiritual and religious. This made it possible, as the years went by, to put
together a picture of Mother Julia, a picture portraying the features of
someone defined by a religious motivation [...] .

Looked at more closely, a deeper reason for the attractiveness of this
religious discussion comes to light: it was saturated with the words and
content of Sacred Scripture. This simple woman, without the benefit of a
university education, had an extraordinary knowledge of Scripture. Her
talk was usually interlaced with striking allusions to the Old and New
Testaments, examples from Biblical history, and texts from the prophets
and Wisdom literature. It would not be misleading to say that her manner
of religious discourse bore the imprint of Biblical wisdom. At the same
time, it fostered profound theological ideas, not in the form of scientific
theology, but in the style of the spiritually animated theology of the saints.
Proof of this assertion can be found in the writings of Mother Julia. They
provide documentary evidence of her unpretentious way of expressing

---

[1] L. Scheffczyk, *Die geistige Gestalt Mutter Julias*. Begegnungen, Bregenz: privately printed by the Spiritual
Family The Work 1999.

herself, though the simplicity goes hand in hand with a wealth of ideas and insights […] .

Preoccupied though they were with the world of faith and the eternal things of salvation, spirituality, and asceticism, the conversations also gave much attention to earthly reality, to history and the present day. For all her engagement with the abiding substance of faith and piety, and for all her joy in the spiritual things that lie beyond time, Mother Julia displayed a pronounced and heartfelt attachment to earthly reality. This explains the energetic way in which she walked with the Church on the journey through history and the present day and shared the Church's experience and fate in the world. She had a particularly close bond with the primitive Church. For her, the mighty representative of this period was St Paul, whose glowing breath wafted through her spiritual character […] .

As regards her relationship with the Church, Mother Julia's spiritual character can be described in a phrase of the ecclesiastical author, Origen, who died in 254. He characterizes the Christian, in both origin and end, as an *anima ecclesiastica*, an *ecclesial* soul. Christ's Mystical Body, which is the Church, comes into the lives of Christians as a mysterious doctrine and soars ahead of them as a high ideal, but on Mother Julia it made its mark on the very texture of her earthly existence. Again and again in conversation, she tried to express what it meant for her. *"I was drawn in a most profound way to a conversion and purification of my whole being. This enabled me to fulfil my mission as a member of the Mystical Body of Christ in fidelity to his light."* [2] And so, looking back on her life, she could say: *"I believe I can make this testimony: my whole life has become a* communio *with the Mystical Body of Christ."* [3]

Christ as Head of the Church, the faithful as His members, the 'circulation' of the 'blood' of grace among the members, enabling them to stand in for one another, to make sacrifices and suffer for each other: you always sensed that for Mother Julia these truths were not just a conceptual theory, a timeless idea. No, for her they had become a concrete reality: she had experienced them in her life. The image of the Church as *communio* was alive in her. Whenever she spoke of Christ the King or Mother Church, of the bridal soul or the family of God, you felt almost tangibly that these words were a living echo from the depths of her being, and, when you heard them, they set up spiritual vibrations in you as well.

---

[2] Mother Julia's Notes, 18 January 1986.
[3] Letter of Mother Julia, 18 January 1985.

On closer familiarity with Mother Julia, supplemented through acquaintance with her written statements and notes, the author gained an insight into the original inspiration and development of this spirituality and *ecclesial* imprinting of the soul. As so often with gifts of the religious and spiritual order, they have their roots in the recipient's unique natural temperament, as created by God, and therefore ultimately they defy any attempt to explain them or show where they come from. However, as with other comparable cases of vocation, when you attempt an explanation, you come across external conditions and circumstances that fostered the unfolding and growth of the gift. In Mother Julia's youth, part of this unfolding were new developments in the life of the Church in Belgium and the Netherlands. These led, in the framework of Catholic Action, to a religious movement of the laity that had a surprising influence on public life and produced an upturn in the life of faith, though any prudent observer at the time would have recognized that it carried with it much that was dangerous. The young woman, already moved by a special grace, recognized acutely that the youthful leadership of Catholic Action was in urgent need of deeper formation, and her director, who was soundly trained in spirituality, confirmed her judgement. At the same time they were both able to see that many of the activities of the movement were less suitable to her personal cast of mind and that, objectively, the external activism, the increasingly this-worldly orientation of the goals the activists set themselves, and the self-confident striving for success in the lives of so many of them were not serving the goal of developing an authentic Christian life.

In her spiritual confrontation with the ambivalence of this situation of her times, there grew in the young woman a fundamental attitude that one might describe simply as a striving for Catholic authenticity. This became more and more clearly the primary concern in the life and mission of Mother Julia: the preservation in all its purity of Catholic faith in conformity to the authentic confession of that faith by the Church. Conversations with her attested in many different ways to this aspiration. The charism given her of a limpid and faith-penetrated awareness of truth enabled her to make, and often to use, the distinction between 'absolute truth' and 'relative truths'. By the latter, she meant the 'opinions' of the day, clouded as they were by subjective self-will and the impure interests of individuals. Her commitment to the truth of the faith was inseparable from the integrity, grounded in conscience, with which she thought and lived in the Church. This meant sincerely living out one's union with Christ by grace, manifested outwardly and visibly in a treasuring of the Sacraments and devotion to the Word of God. It also meant intellectual commitment to dogma and the teaching of the Church. In Mother Julia, from a very early period, life and truth formed an indestructible unity in a vitality of faith that had its roots in a piety of the heart but also of consciousness of the truth.

The rooting of this specifically *ecclesial* piety in a faith internalized and resounding in the heart gives the possibility of understanding how an existentially and personally very intense form of devotion to Christ took hold of Mother Foundress at the time of her religious maturity. It was inherent in devotion to the Sacred Heart, which was promoted especially by the two Popes, Pius XI and XII. It is not hard to see why a living and ardent faith in Christ, of the kind Mother Julia had, should be specially drawn to the Sacred Heart of Jesus, which is not only the supreme expression of our Lord's divine and human love for mankind and each individual human being, but also the most powerful motivation of man's love for the Redeemer. Veneration of the Sacred Heart of Jesus presented the *anima ecclesiastica* of Mother Julia with a devotion that would afford the deepest expression to the Church's identity as loving and obedient *communio* with her redeeming Head. For her this devotion meant the possibility of a two-way relationship of the utmost interiority, with the person and continuing work of Jesus Christ and was therefore a most delightful grace. However, it was also a supreme responsibility and vocation. She perceived within it the call to a total gift of self to the Redeemer and to apostolic participation in His redeeming work through sacrifice of one's own heart and life.

From the broken Heart of Jesus Christ she also learnt the obligation of suffering and the Cross in the life of the person called. This obligation she passed on to her community, and she gave solemn expression to it in the emblem of the radiant crown of thorns. What she said in conversation about these things, she has put down in writing in many luminous texts. For example, she made this confession: "*In Christ's Passion, the Precious Blood poured out of His pierced Heart and now flows in the Eucharistic Sacrifice. In His light, my soul was plunged into the mystery. I was able to experience more deeply the gift of His inexpressibly merciful love, which has invited us to make a 'Holy Covenant' binding us to His Heart so full of mercy and justice.*" [4]

---

[4] Letter of Mother Julia, 30 July 1985.

If the Church as Christ's Mystical Body was the spiritual place where she lived, the Heart of Jesus represented the innermost sanctuary of that place. *"My heart has found a place to dwell. Where Jesus my Beloved dwells, there my soul is filled with peace and joy; these are the gifts of Jesus, who is really present. I want to abide in the wound in His side, hidden in His Heart, in order with Him to share His life as Redeemer and to lead, in many different ways, a hidden life."* [5]

The lofty theological analogy of the Body of Christ was complemented, on the practical side and for application to daily living, in the image of the Church as *communio* and 'family of God'. Long before Vatican II, and afterwards more vigorously through reception of the Council, Mother Julia took up these two concepts in her religious thought and developed them as points of reference for shaping the life not only of the individual but also of the community, The Work. Needless to say, *communio* was not understood in a merely horizontal way and reduced to life with one's fellow men. No, it was given its vertical dimension, and, as the Foundress of The Work occasionally said, it was related to the 'Three Churches': *"We must once again see, experience, and live in union with the Three Churches, the Church Militant, Suffering, and Triumphant, in their complementarity. What beauty, what richness lies in this mystery!"* [6]

All these elements distinguishing Mother Julia's spiritual character carried over into her view of the community she founded, which again and again became the topic of conversation. After a time, having become familiar with her religious and spiritual disposition, her interlocutor came to take it for granted that this charismatically gifted woman was created expressly for the formation of a religious community. But soon he was also allowed to make himself familiar with the special characteristic of this vocation, which was to a high degree detached from self-assertion and self-will. What brings out the specifically *ecclesial* and hierarchical nature of her foundation is the fact that Julia Verhaeghe entrusted herself to the priest, who was her spiritual director, and that on 18th January 1938 her 'Holy Covenant with the Heart of Jesus' [7] was united with the priest's own. She saw this spiritual bond, which was established in the Week of Prayer for Christian Unity, as a strengthening of the *ecclesial* bond, where charism and hierarchical office, laity and priesthood are related to one

---

[5] Letter of Mother Julia, 9 August 1980.
[6] Conversation with Mother Julia, 14 November 1984.
[7] Mother Julia's grace of the "Holy Covenant" was on the Feast of the Sacred Heart of Jesus 1934.

another and where in the complementarity with which this community is filled, the life of the Church, turned towards the Heart of Jesus, becomes a more intense reality. In fact, this bond constituted the first cell of The Work, which was afterwards to expand, as from itself, into a growing organism. The essential elements of the charism were established in the community's origin: making the Church visible as the family of faith in the strength of complementarity, of which the inter-dependence of priests and women consecrated to God is one instance […] .

For Mother Julia, the liturgy was the privileged place in which the faith manifests itself as the objective expression of the Church's worship of God and the Church's creed. She herself entered into it with deepest emotion, and she bequeathed the reverent celebration of the liturgy as a permanent prescription for the community. In matters of religion and faith, reverence was one of Mother Julia's fundamental principles; it informed the whole attitude and direction of her life and passed from her into the community.

As in the early Church, Mother Julia regarded tireless zeal for the purity of faith as the *virginity* of faith, and she explained it by analogy with the virginity of the Mother of God. In a special way, she applied it to the Church of today. The sensitivity of her vocation to the present-day situations can be regarded as one of the distinguishing characteristics of her apostolic outlook; indeed, it is to be seen as a criterion of the authenticity of her entire mission.

Important Dates in the life of Mother Julia

1910	11 November	Julia Verhaeghe is born in Geluwe (Belgium) the eighth of eleven children of Henri Verhaeghe and Valentine Rosé
1910	13 November	Baptism in the parish church
1912	1 June	Ordination to the priesthood of Fr Hillewaere in Bruges
1914	3 August	The First World War begins
1917	October	The Verhaeghe family flees to Lembeek near Halle
between 1917 and 1920		Begins primary school in Lembeek, first confession and first Commuinon
1918	11 November	The First World War ends
1920	March	The Verhaeghe family returns to Geluwe
1920 - 1924		Attends primary school
1922	15 June	'Solemn communion' with renewal of baptismal vows
1922		Becomes member of Eucharistic Crusade
1922	12 September	Arthur Cyriel Hillewaere is appointed curate in Geluwe
1923	15 September	The Verhaeghe family moves into the new house in Geluwe
1924	8 July	Confirmation in the parish church
1924 - 1930		Works in the service of various families in Belgium and France
between 1925 and 1926		Receives missal, encounter with St Paul
1928		Stays at the sea in Het Zoute-aan-Zee
1929	March	Goes to the film "The King of Kings" in Kortrijk
1929	March	Falls downs the stairs

1930	10 January	Becomes member of the 'apostolate for the sick'
1930 - 1941		Years of sickness at her parents' house, takes up needle work
1934	11 February	Becomes member of the third order of Carmelites
1934	8 June	Grace of the 'Holy Covenant' on the feast of the Sacred Heart
1935	16 December	Death of her mother
1937	14 February	Death of her father
1938	18 January	Birthday of The Work, "Holy Covenant" of Fr Hillewaere, Julia's new mission as Mother of The Work
1938	30 September	The Bishop of Bruges is informed of The Work
1938 - 1941		First development of the charism, some young women offer up their sufferings for the growth of The Work
1939	1 September	The Second World War begins
1939	19 October	Fr Hillewaere is appointed parish priest in Komen-ten-Brielen
1940	10 May	Germany invades Belgium
1940	14 - 18 May	Canon Cardijn and his co-operators in Komen-ten-Brielen
1940	28 May	Belgium surrenders, beginning of German occupation
1941	16 July	Leaves her parents' home, works in Sint-Niklaas, accompanies the first vocations
1941	12 November	Goes to work in Kortrijk and begins her apostolate among young women in domestic service
1942	30 September	Returns to Geluwe to nurse her sick sister Madeleine
1943	12 February	Fr Hillewaere is appointed parish priest of St Joseph in Menin
1943	24 September	Journey to Brussels, concern for unity
1943	23 November	Death of Julia's sister Madeleine

1944	4 July	Returns to Geluwe, again ill
1944	September	Liberation of Belgium through the allies
1944 - 1946		Julia returns to Sint-Niklaas, formation of first vocations, domestic service, work in two factories, interruptions through illness
1945	8 May	Signing of capitulation documents in Berlin, the Second World War ends
1945	1 - 4 November	First communal retreat
1946	7 - 8 December	Days of recollection in Menin, meeting at Fr Hillewaere's, decision for a common life
1947	9 April	Start of common life in Sint-Niklaas
1948	6 January	Move to a new house in Brussels (Ducpétiauxlaan)
1948	August	Start of co-operation of The Work with the 'Women's Association of the Christian Worker Movement'
1949	15 March	Fr Hillewaere is appointed parish parist in Zwevegem
1949	19 March	Foundation of the state recognised association 'Paulusheim'
1949	3 August	Beginning of a new house in Wezembeek near Brussels
1950	Mai	Move to a bigger house in Brussels (Bollandisten Street) as home for the training of the family assistants
1950	15 May	Move to the convent in Villers-Notre-Dame
1950	July	Visit of His Lordship Mgr Charles-Marie Himmer, bishop of Tournai, to Villers-Notre-Dame. Meeting with Mother Julia
1950	Autumn	State authorisation of the own fully independent family assistance service, beginning of a new development
1950	Autumn	Definite separation from Catholic Action
1950	29 - 31 October	Triduum to prepare for the entry of the Eucharistic Lord into the chapel of Villers-Notre-Dame

BIBLIOGRAPHY

1. *Published Sources*

L. ALAERTS, *Door eigen werk sterk*. Geschiedenis van de kajotters en kajotsters in Vlaanderen 1924-1967, Leuven: Kadoc - Kajottershuis 2004.

ANON., *La catastrophe de chemin de fer de Lembecq,* in: *L'Evénement lllustré 5 (*17 juillet 1919/195) 379.

ANON., *La journée du centenaire,* in: *La Feuille.* Bulletin d'informations des papeteries Dalle et Lecomte Bousbecque, Numéro spécial du Centenaire (Octobre 1979/3*).*

E. ARNOULD, A. BOULVIN, L. BRAGARD et al, (Eds.), *Va libérer mon peuple! (Ex 3:10).* La pensée de Joseph Cardijn, Paris-Bruxelles: Editions Ouvrières-Vie Ouvrière 1982.

R. AUBERT, *Das Erwachen der katholischen Lebenskraft,* in: Handbuch der Kirchengeschichte, Vol. VI/1: Die Kirche zwischen Revolution and Restauration, ed. H. Jedin, Freiburg-Basel-Wien: Herder 1971, 247-259, 272-310.

R. AUBERT, *Der Ausbruch des 1. Weltkriegs,* in: Handbuch der Kirchengeschichte, Vol. VI/2: Die Kirche zwischen Anpassung und Widerstand, 1878 bis 1914, ed. H. Jedin, Freiburg-Basel-Wien: Herder 1973, 538-545.

R. AUBERT, *Die erste Phase des katholischen Liberalismus,* in: Handbuch der Kirchengeschichte, Vol. VI/1: Die Kirche zwischen Revolution und Restauration, ed. H. Jedin, Freiburg-Basel-Wien: Herder 1971, 320-414.

Belgisch Staatsblad/Moniteur belge, 19 March 1949, Dossier No. 706.

D. BERAT, G. HOUWEN, *Derde Eeuwfeest van het Sint-Stanislascollege te Poperinge. Historisch overzicht 1657-1957,* Poperinge: privately printed 1957.

K. BERQUIN, *De dringende noodzakelijkheid van E.K.,* Averbode: Goede Pers-Altoria 1948.

R. BOUDENS, *De Kerk in Vlaanderen.* Momentopnamen, Averbode-Apeldoorn: Altoria 1994.

R. BOUDENS, *Henri Lamiroy (1931-1952),* in: *Het bisdom Brugge (1559-1984). Bisschoppen, priesters, gelovigen,* ed. M. Cloet, Bruges: privately printed by Westvlaams Verbond van kringen voor heemkunde [2]1985, 389-400.

J. CARDIJN, *Jeunes travailleurs face aux temps nouveaux,* Bruxelles: Editions Jocistes 1942.

J. CARDIJN, *Le problème de la jeunesse,* Bruxelles 1943.

J. CARDIJN, *Leken in de voorste linie. Laïcs en première ligne,* Brussels: D.A.P. Sociale uitgaven 1964.

J. CARDIJN, *Op zijn tijd vooruit: historische en profetische gedachten: 200 artikels verschenen in la Cité 1950-1963,* Merchtem 1980.

J. CASSART, *Les Madones anciennes du diocèse de Tournai,* in: Revue Diocésaine de Tournai (November 1954), without page number.

M. CLOET, (Ed.), *Het bisdom Brugge (1559-1984). Bisschoppen, priesters, gelovigen,* Bruges: privately printed by Westvlaams Verbond van kringen voor heemkunde [2]1985.

W. DE BROUWER (Ed.), *Geschiedenis van de kleine Man,* Brussels: BRT - Open School 1979 (this book is part of a multimedia project including 14 television programmes and 7 radio programmes).

D. DE KEYZER, *"Madame est servie". Leven in dienst van adel en burgerij (1900-1995),* Leuven: Van Halewyck [5]1996.

A. DEBUF, D. DECUYPERE, H. DRIESSENS, J. DURNEZ, M. GHEKIERE, M. LAMBRECHT, *Geluwe, zo was het...,* Geluwe: privately printed by Plaatselijke Openbare Bibliotheek [2]1985.

D. DECUYPERE, *Dorp zonder grenzen. 1940-1945 - epicentrum Geluwe,* Geluwe: privately printed 1985.

D. DECUYPERE, *Geluwnaren van taal en gemoed. Aspecten van een eeuw Vlaams denken op of vanuit Geluwe. 50 jaar Davidsfonds op Geluwe (1931-1981),* Geluwe: Davidsfonds 1981.

D. DECUYPERE, *Het malheur van de keizer. Geluwe 1914-1918,* Geluwe: privately printed 1998.

R. DEJONGHE, A. DE MOFFARTS, C. PETIT, D. VANDENPLAS, E. VANNEROM, R. WRIGHT, *De Familie Claes. Van landbouwers tot industriëlen en grootgrondbezitters - Lembeek van de 17de tot de 19de eeuw,* Halle: privately printed by Koninklijke Geschied- en Oudheidkundige Kring 1987.

S. DESODT, *Geen rijker kroon dan eigen schoon. Onze Lieve Vrouw van Dadizele,* Dadizele: privately printed, no date.

A. DONDEYNE, *Net wereldcongres op het Heizelstadion,* in: *Universitas 2* (october 1935).

A. DONDEYNE, *Geloven wij nog in de KAJ?,* in: *Op de voorposten! Verslag van de nationale studieweek voor eerw. Heren proosten van KAJ en VKAJ, to Mechelen 1947,* Mechelen 1948, 7-24.

H. DRIESSENS, *Wij zijn samen onderweg...*, in: *Geluwe - Sint-Dionysius,* Weekblad, 50 (13 January 1972) 1.

K. DUBOIS, L, ENGELEN, *Katholieke Actie voor de Jeugd in Vlaanderen,* Antwerpen: JVKA-Uitgaven 1928.

W. DUMONT, *Fenomenologie van de massamanifestaties in België in de jaren dertig*; in: *Belgisch Tijdschrift voor Nieuwste Geschiedenis, 29* (1999) 12, 145-266.

J. DURNEZ, *Over 't Roosetje en zijn bewoners ...*, Geluwe: privately printed 1983.

C. ESTEBAN, A. MUHLSTEIN, (Eds.), *Grootboek van de Tweede Wereldoorlog,* first part: *Van München tot Pearl Harbor,* Amsterdam-Brussels: The Reader's Digest 1966.

H. FAELENS *Front 14/18 langs de Ijzer-Parcours,* Brussels: Artis-Historia 1993.

M. FIEVEZ, J. MEERT, *Cardijn,* avec la collaboration de R. Aubert, Bruxelles: Vie Ouvrière [3]1978.

N. FISCHER, *Chronik 1914. Tag für Tag in Wort und Bild,* Die Chronik-Bibliothek des 20. Jahrhunderts, Vol. 14, ed. B. Harenberg, Dortmund: Chronik-Verlag [2]1989.

T. FLEMMING, A. STEINHAGE, P. STRUNK, *Chronik 1945. Tag für Tag in Wort und Bild,* Die Chronik-Bibliothek des 20. Jahrhunderts, Vol. 45, ed. B. Harenberg, Dortmund: Chronik-Verlag [3]1994.

E. GERARD (Ed.), *De christelijke arbeidersbeweging in België,* Deel 2 (Kadoc-Studies 11), Leuven: Universitaire Pers 1991.

R.J. GILLET (Ed.), *Historie van het Zoute-kerkje 1925-1975,* Knokke-Heist: Paters Dominikanen 1974.

Hallensia. Bulletin van de Koninklijke Geschied- en Oudheidkundige Kring van Halle, Nieuwe Reeks, 1 (April-June 1979/2).

J. HARTMANN, *Das Geschichtsbuch. Von den Anfängen bis zur Gegenwart* (Fischer Taschenbücher 6314), Frankfurt: Fischer-Bücherei 1966.

W. HOFER, *Die Entfesselung des Zweiten Weltkrieges. Eine Studie über die internationalen Beziehungen im Sommer 1939 mit Dokumenten,* Frankfurt: Fischer-Bücherei 1960.

K. HOFMANN, *Eucharistischer Kinderkreuzzug,* in: Lexikon für Theologie und Kirche, Vol. 3, ed. J. Hofer and K. Rahner, Freiburg: Herder [2]1959, 1165.

C. HÜNERMANN, *Chronik 1941. Tag für Tag in Wort und Bild,* Die

Chronik-Bibliothek des 20. Jahrhunderts, Vol. 41, ed. B. Harenberg, Gütersloh-München: Chronik im Bertelsmann Lexikon Verlag 2001.

E. HUYS, *Geschiedenis van Geluwe,* met aanvullingen door D. Decuypere, Geluwe: privately printed by Luc Demeester [3]1977.

INTERDIOCESAAN CENTRUM (Ed.), *Katholiek Jaarboek voor België,* Brussels: privately printed 1958.

E. ISERLOH, *Innerkirchliche Bewegungen und ihre Spiritualität,* in: Handbuch der Kirchengeschichte, Vol. VII: Die Weltkirche im 20. Jahrhundert, ed. H. Jedin and K. Repgen, Freiburg-Basel-Wien: Herder 1979, 301-337.

H. JEDIN, K. REPGEN, (Eds.), *Die Weltkirche im 20. Jahrhundert,* Handbuch der Kirchengeschichte, Vol. VII, Freiburg-Basel-Wien: Herder 1979.

JOHN PAUL II, Apostolisches Schreiben *Novo millennio ineunte,* Vatican City: Libreria Editrice Vaticana 2001.

J. KERKHOFS, J. VAN HOUTTE (Eds.), *De Kerk in Vlaanderen. Pastoraal-sociologische studie van het leven en de structuur der Kerk,* Tielt-Den Haag: Lanoo 1962.

F. KOLBE, *Die liturgische Bewegung,* in: Der Christ in der Welt. Eine Enzyklopadie, Vol. IX/4, ed. J. Hirschmann, Aschaffenburg: Pattloch 1964.

J. LEGRAND, *Chronique du 20ᵉ siècle,* Paris: Chronique [2]1987.

J. LESCRAUWAET, *Gebedsweek,* in: Liturgisch Woordenboek, ed. L. Brinkhof, G. C. Laudy, A. Verheul, Th. A. Vismans, W. De Wolf, Roermond/Maaseik: J. J. Romen & Zonen 1958-1962.

K. LIEBAERT, *De Dominicanenkerk in het Zoute,* Brugge: Van De Wiele 2003.

J. LOGIE, *Geluwe en zijn kerk,* in: *De gidsenkring,* Westland-nummer 30 (February 1992).

R. ORROI, *Archief College: Leerkrachten Lagere School - School voor aangepast onderwijs - Secundaire school 1657-2001,* Poperinge: Sint-Stanislas College 2001 (archief.college.poperinge@sip.be).

A. OSAER, *De christelijke arbeidersvrouwenbeweging,* in: De christelijke arbeidersbeweging in België (Kadoc-Studies 11), ed. E. Gerard, Leuven: Universitaire Pers 1991, 317-411.

A. PALMER, H. THOMAS, *Die Moderne Welt im Aufbruch,* Meilensteine der Geschichte, Vol. III, translated by S. Erbe, S. De Gaspere, S. Hammer et al., Frankfurt-Berlin: Ullstein 1972.

PIUS XII, *Discorsi e Radiomessaggi, vol.* XII, Città del Vaticano: Tipografia Poliglotta Vaticana 1955.

PIUS XII, *Radiobotschaft an die "Christliche Arbeiterjugend" (JOC) Belgiens vom 3.* September 1950, in: *Aufbau and Entfaltung des gesellschaftlichen Lebens.* Soziale Summe Pius XII., Vol. 2, ed. A.-F. Utz and J.-F. Groner, Freiburg/Schweiz: Paulusverlag 1954, Nos. 2956-2964.

PIUS XII, *The Mystical Body of Christ*, Catholic Truth Society, London 1943.

B. POLMANN, *Chronik 1934. Tag für Tag in Wort und Bild*, Die Chronik-Bibliothek des 20. Jahrhunderts, Vol. 34, ed. B. Harenberg, Dortmund: Chronik-Verlag ³1993.

S. REINHARDT, *Chronik 1917. Tag für Tag in Wort und Bild*, Die Chronik-Bibliothek des 20. Jahrhunderts, Vol. 17, ed. B. Harenberg, Dortmund: Chronik-Verlag ³1991.

S. REINHARDT, *Chronik 1918. Tag für Tag in Wort und Bild*, Die Chronik-Bibliothek des 20. Jahrhunderts, Vol. 18, ed. B. Harenberg, Dortmund: Chronik-Verlag ²1988.

S. de SCHAEPDRIJVER, *De Groote Oorlog. Het koninkrijk België tijdens de Eerste Wereldoorlog*, without place: Olympus-Contact ⁵1999.

A. SCHEUCHER, A. WALD, H. LEIN, E. STAUDINGER, *Vom Beginn des Industriezeitalters bis zum Zweiten Weltkrieg*, Zeitbilder, Geschichte und Sozialkunde, Vol. 7: Vienna: öbv & hpt ²1999.

B. SCHINDLER, *Chronik 1940. Tag für Tag in Wort and Bild*, Die Chronik-Bibliothek des 20. Jahrhunderts, Vol. 40, ed. B. Harenberg, Dortmund: Chronik-Verlag ²1990.

E.C. SCHÜTT, *Chronik 1933. Tag für Tag in Wort and Bild*, Die Chronik-Bibliothek des 20. Jahrhunderts, Vol. 33, ed. B. Harenberg, Dortmund: Chronik-Verlag ²1993.

E.C. SCHÜTT, *Chronik 1938. Tag für Tag in Wort and Bild*, Die Chronik-Bibliothek des 20. Jahrhunderts, Vol. 38, ed. B. Harenberg, Dortmund: Chronik-Verlag 1988.

P. TAGHON, *Mei 40.* De achttiendaagse veldtocht in België, Tielt: Lannoo 1989.

K. VAN ISACKER, *De enge ruimte 1914-1980,* Mijn land in de kering, 1830-1980, Deel 2, Antwerpen-Amsterdam: De Nederlandsche Boekhandel 1983.

M. VAN ROEY, *Cardijn,* Brussels: Reinaert 1972.

M. VANDENBULCKE, *Arthur Hillewaere: een merkwaardig priester,* in:

Negentiende Jaarboek van de Heemkundige Kring Karel Van de Poele te Lichtervelde, 19 (2003) 195-199.

J. VERSCHEURE, *Katholische Aktion,* in: Lexikon für Theologie und Kirche, ed. J. Hofer and K. Rahner, Vol. 6, Freiburg: Herder '1961, 902ff.

L. VOS, *Les paroisses et les Curés du diocèse actuel de Tournai,* Vol. VII, Bruges: Desclée de Brouwer et Cie 1903.

L. VOS, P. WYNANTS, A. TIHON, *De christelijke arbeidersjeugd* in: De christelijke arbeidersbeweging in België (Kadoc-Studies 11), ed. E. Gerard, Leuven: Universitaire Pers 1991, 413-479.

L. VOS, *De Eerste Wereldoorlog,* Leuven: Davidsfonds ⁵2003.

2. *Unpublished Sources*

THE SPIRITUAL FAMILY THE WORK, Private Archives Bregenz-Thalbach

ARCHAEOLOGICAL ARCHIVES OF WERVIK

ARCHIVES GENERALES DU ROYAUME, "Fonds-Cardijn". To this part of the archive there are two inventories: M. FIEVEZ, F. WINDELS-ROSART, *Inventaris van het Fonds-Cardijn,* ed. Ministerie van onderwijs en Ministère de l'éducation nationale, Algemeen Rijksarchief en Rijksarchief in de Provincies, translated by C. De Cuyper and K. Goris, Brussels: privately printed by Algemeen Rijksarchief, 1986. M. FIEVEZ, A. BRICTEUX, A. ERICX, *Complément à l'inventaire Cardijn* (Archives générales du Royaume instruments de recherche à tirage limité 409), Brussels: privately printed by Archives générales du Royaume 1996.

ARCHIVES OF JUNIOR SEMINARY, Roeselaere.

ARCHIVES OF THE CATHOLIC WORKERS' MOVEMENT, Brussels.

P. BENTEIN, Private Archives, Geluwe.

P. BOYCE, Der Segen, Bregenz: privately printed by The Spiritual Family The Work 1981.

CHRISTIAN BROTHERS, Archives de la Maison Généralice, Rome; Archives in Groot-Bijgarden (Belgium).

DIOCESE OF BRUGES, Diocesan Archives.

DISCALCED CARMELITES, Archives of the Province, Carmel, Ghent.

J. DURNEZ, Private Archives, Waregem.

A. FLAMENT, Private Archives, Geluwe.

GELUWE ARCHIVES

GELUWE PARISH ARCHIVES

HALLE ARCHIVES

HISTORICAL STUDY CIRCLE KOMEN-TEN-BRIELEN

KNOKKE ARCHIVES

KOMEN-TEN-BRIELEN PARISH ARCHIVES, "Anno 1940".

KORTRIJK ARCHIVES

LEMBEEK ARCHIVES

LEMBEEK PARISH ARCHIVES

LICHTERVELDE ARCHIVES

MENIN ARCHIVES

MENIN PARISH ARCHIVES

MINISTRY OF FINANCE, *Administration de l'enregistrement et des domaines.* Direction à Bruges, Conservation à Ypres, Registre de transcription 1921.

MINISTRY OF FINANCE, *Beheer der registratie en domeinen*, Bestuur Brugge, Grondpandbewaring Yperen, Aanwijzingregister der hypothecaire formaliteiten 1923.

L. MORLION, Private Archives, Geluwe.

POPPERINGE ARCHIVES

L. SCHEFFCZYK, *Die geistige Gestalt Mutter Julias.* Begegnungen, Bregenz: privately printed by The Spiritual Family The Work 1999.

SINT-NIKLAAS ARCHIVES

TOURCOING ARCHIVES

VANNEROM E., Private Archives, Lembeek.

WERVIK ARCHIVES

YPRES ARCHIVES

ZWEVEGEM ARCHIVES

ZWEVEGEM PARISH ARCHIVES

Memorabilia in private hands of relatives and friends of Mother Julia Verhaeghe and Fr Arthur Cyriel Hillewaere.

Memories and testimonies of relatives and friends of Mother Julia Verhaeghe and Fr Arthur Cyriel Hillewaere.

SOURCES OF PICTURES

The editors thank all who kindly provided pictures and documents or gave permission for them to be printed.

Archives of the Benedictine Abbey of Affligem (Belgium)   54

Archives of the Dominican Fathers and Archives of Kristine Liebaert,
    Knokke-Het-Zoute (Belgium)   61, 62

Bailleur Roger, Wervik (Belgium)   33

Basilica Santa Cecilia, Rome   6

Diocese of Bruges, Diocesan Archives   101

Decoene Daisy for the "Heemkundige Kring Dadingisila",
    Dadizele (Belgium)   31

Decuypere Dirk (Ed.), *Dorp zonder grenzen. 1940-1945 - epicentrum Geluwe*,
    Geluwe: privately printed 1985   107

Decuypere Dirk, *Geluwnaren van taal en gemoed. Aspecten van een
eeuw Vlaams denken op of vanuit Geluwe*. 50 jaar Davidsfonds op
    Geluwe (1931-1981), Geluwe: Davidsfonds 1981   34

Delforge Frédéric, Leuze-en-Hainaut (Belgium)   167

Dewaele-Morlion Anne, Geluwe (Belgium)   49

Film *The King of Kings*, directed by Cecil B. De Mille, U.S.A. 1927   65, 66, 67

Güfel Josef, Feldkirch (Austria)   125

Huys Emiel, *Geschiedenis van Geluwe,* met aanvullingen door D.
    Decuypere, Geluwe, privately printed by Luc Demeester [3]1977   29, 45

Lestienne-Cordonnier Françoise, Montpellier (France)   70

Marchand Guido for the Geluwe parish archives (Belgium)   30

Menin Archives (Belgium)   41

Modica Vincenzo, Rome   16

L'Osservatore Romano, photo service, Rome   84

Pinoy Franc, Geluwe (Belgium)   46

Rousseau Michael, Geluwe (Belgium)   55

Town Council of Sint-Niklaas, *Archivaria 2* (November 1994) 73   134

Vannerom Emile, Lembeek (Belgium)   41

Van Hoonacker E., *Kortrijk in oude prentkaarten*, Zaltbommel (Netherlands):
    Europese Bibliotheek [6]2000, picture No 137   117

Wijnants Christian, Brussels   148

All illustrations, documents and drawings which are not listed are in the private archives of The Spiritual Family The Work, Thalbach in Bregenz, Austria or were provided by persons who required no attribution.